the new tea companion

a guide to teas throughout the world

JANE PETTIGREW & BRUCE RICHARDSON

First published in the USA in 2008 by Benjamin Press

Benjamin Press
PO Box 100
Perryville, Kentucky 40468 USA
800.765.2139
www.benjaminpress.com

Reproduction by Rival Colour Ltd, UK
Printed and bound by Craft Print Ltd, Singapore

ISBN 978-0-9793431-7-9

Published in the United Kingdom in 2008 by
National Trust Books
10 Southcombe Street
London W14 0RA

An imprint of Anova Books Company Ltd

Picture Acknowledgements
Jane and Bruce would like to say a very sincere thank you to the following friends who have kindly allowed the use of their photographs in this book: Tim d'Offay, UK pages 37, 57, 171, 212, 217, 243; Mr and Mrs Fukunaga, Japan: page 242; Ambootia Tea Estate, India pages 32, 45, 52, 53; Teloijan Tea Brokers, India page 46 (right) ; Jaewon Won, Korea pages 33, 185, 186, 187, 240; The Tao of Tea, USA pages 229, 230; Nigel Melican, Teacraft, UK pages 35, 36, 147, 227; Roberto Navajas, Argentina pages 37, 235; Maurice Levy, USA pages 38, 41, 42 (top), 44, 101, 102, 239 ; R Twinings Ltd pages 42, 46 (left); The UK Tea Council, UK page 59; Tregothnan Tea Estate, UK pages 66, 223, 224; Edward Eisler, UK page 47; Joe Wertheim, Rwanda page 201.

Thanks also to the following: Mary Evans Picture Library pages 8 and 10; National Trust Picture Library pages 13 (© NTPL, by kind permission of the Bedingfeld family), 14 (© NTPL/Bill Batten), 15 (© NTPL/Andreas von Einsiedel), 20 (© NTPL/Derrick E. Witty).

Contents

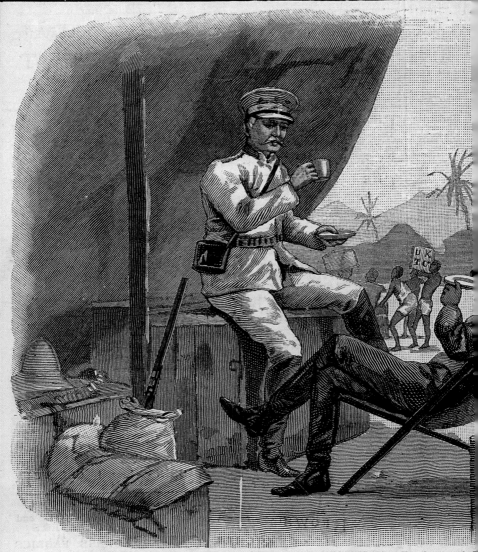

STANLEY: "Well, Emin, old fellow, this Cup of the United Kingdom Tea Company's T
EMIN: "So it does, my boy."

Tea's origins in China

Anyone who has any interest at all in tea, no matter how new or how small, cannot fail to recognize the fascinating links between modern tea-drinking and Ancient China. The story weaves its way so far back through Chinese history (2737BC is the date always mentioned as the starting point) that it is impossible to know the true facts, and so stories and legends have grown up to explain the discovery, early cultivation and consumption of this wonderful life-enhancing beverage. Tea's journey through the ages and across every continent has inevitably meant the gradual development of new production methods, new rituals and new, inventive pieces of equipage, but we cannot deny its colourful and intriguing origins.

The accepted myths and legends tell us that it was Shen Nung, emperor, scholar and herbalist, who first recognized tea's healthful properties and refreshingly delicious taste when a few stray leaves drifted down from an overhanging tree one day and fell by chance into the cauldron of water that he was boiling. Other stories of tea's discovery have been told over the centuries, but all praise tea's ability to alleviate drowsiness and assist concentration, to restore energy, combat depression and revive the spirit. Recognized from the earliest days as a tonic herb, tea was taken internally by the Chinese as a digestive aid and applied topically in ointments to alleviate skin troubles and rheumatism.

During the rule of the Han Dynasty (AD 206–220), tea became more and more popular and today antique lacquer tea trays and tables, decorated lacquer cups and early porcelain tea bowls from the period bear witness to the drink's widespread use. It is thought that until this time wild tea trees had been felled so that the leaves might be stripped off for brewing and, as demand for the raw material grew, plantations were established for commercial cultivation. This, and improved methods of manufacture, helped to guarantee a regular, good-quality crop and allow the growth of a thriving trade throughout China which earned fortunes for the traders.

By the end of the third century AD, tea had become China's national drink and in AD332 the first record of tea manufacture was written by Zhang Yi, giving details of how plants were laid out, pruned and plucked, and how the leaves were processed. During the fourth and fifth centuries, many new plantations were established along the Yangtze River Valley, and tea was now consumed not simply as a tonic brew but as a pleasurable drink. During the Tang Dynasty (AD618–906), a strict code of tea etiquette evolved and a new professional class of Tea Masters acquired an important role in society as employees of the emperor and wealthy mandarins. During the reign of the Song Dynasty (AD960–1279), the Chinese Tea-house became the focus of Chinese social life and a venue for merchants and dealers, friends and families, to gather and talk business, chat, relax, play cards or chess, and enjoy the professional storytellers, poets, jugglers and actors who entertained there.

During the eighth century AD, LuYu, China's first real tea specialist and known today as 'the patron saint of tea', wrote his *Cha Chang* (Classic of Tea). Having learnt how to brew tea correctly from his adoptive father, a Buddhist monk, LuYu worked for 20 years to produce a work that became essential reading for tea farmers, tea merchants and the consuming Chinese public. In the *Cha Chang* he described the plant and its cultivation, the way in which different teas are manufactured, instructed readers as to what sort of water to use for brewing, and examined the culture and rituals of tea-drinking, and the health benefits that make it a perfect beverage.

The Chinese were by now trading their tea to Tibet and the Arab lands to the West, to the Turks, to tribes and groups living in the Himalayas and along the 'Silk Road' trading route that linked India to Macedonia. Trade with Europe started in the late sixteenth century but the long sea voyages often resulted in deterioration of the tea and forced the Chinese tea producers to find ways of improving manufacture, packaging and transportation. Until this point in tea's history, all Chinese teas were green and under the Ming Dynasty (AD1368–1644), instead of being formed into dried compressed cakes as in previous times, the delicate dried leaf was sold loose and consequently was easily spoiled before it reached the customer. So the profit-conscious Chinese producers devised a method of manufacturing black teas. This meant that the leaf lasted longer and travelled better. To make black tea they allowed the leaves to oxidize naturally before drying them to a dark coppery colour. The Chinese people continued to drink green tea but the new black variety found burgeoning markets as European trading companies imported increasing supplies to their home ports.

How the Chinese drank their tea

Until the third century AD, under the Han Dynasty (AD206–220) the Chinese drank tea as a medicinal tonic brew made from the freshly gathered leaves of the wild tea tree. For the next 700 or so years, the plucked leaves were steamed and then compressed into tightly packed cakes of different forms which could be easily stored or transported with minimum damage. To brew tea from these cakes, the brick or cake was roasted and then chopped or crushed, and steeped or boiled in hot water. The infusion was then often flavoured with sweet onions, salt, ginger, orange peel, cloves or mint.

During the days of the Song Dynasty (AD960–1279), the compressed cakes developed a characteristic triangular shape and were crushed and steeped in the same way, but spicy flavouring was now abandoned in favour of gentler additions such as jasmine, lotus and chrysanthemum flowers. It was during this period that powdered tea also became popular.

The gathering of the leaf and the processing of the tea demanded great patience and skill. The young shoots of exclusive bushes were carefully plucked and stored inside airtight jars for several months. The dried leaves were then ground to a fine powder which was whisked into hot water to give a frothy liquid. Depending on the buds that had been gathered, the colour of the whisked tea varied from

Preparing the ground and sewing tea seeds in nineteenth-century China.

exquisite white to a rich jade green. Up to seven fresh additions of water were poured onto the residue of the ground tea to give a different colour and flavour at each whisking.

Under the Ming Dynasty (AD 1368–1644), although some tea was still compressed into cakes and bricks, the fashion for loose tea gradually developed. The leaves were plucked, dried and shaped and then stored loose in sealed earthenware or lacquer chests. To brew the tea, the whole leaves were steeped in boiling water inside earthenware or porcelain teapots – the method of preparation copied by European drinkers when early supplies of the loose tea began to arrive in Amsterdam, Lisbon and London.

Beyond China's borders

It is hard to know when the Mongolians and Tibetans learned to drink tea from the Chinese but it was probably in the second or third century AD. Compressed cakes of dried tea from China were transported by camel and the brew became the national drink of both races. Turkish traders are also recorded as having bartered for tea on the Mongolian border in the late sixth century and today tea is far more important than coffee in Turkey, despite popular belief. Trade with the Arab world started in the fifth and sixth centuries AD but there is no proof that tea was amongst the goods sold until the reign of Kublai Khan in the thirteenth century.

In the eighth century AD, the Japanese discovered the benefits of tea-drinking from the Chinese as a result of contact between Buddhist priests from the two countries. In AD729, the Japanese emperor, Shomu, is said to have served tea to 100 Buddhist monks at his palace in Nara. In the early ninth century, the Buddhist monk Dengyo Daishi carried some tea seeds home with him from China (where he had been studying) and planted them in the garden of his monastery. The plants were carefully tended for five years and then the first harvest of leaves and buds was gathered and used to brew tea for the Emperor Saga. The emperor was apparently so delighted with the beverage that he gave instructions for five plantations to be established for the commercial cultivation of the bushes. Tea became the favourite drink of Japanese Buddhist monks who found that it helped them to stay awake during long periods of prayer and meditation but, due to a cooling in Chinese–Japanese relations from the ninth to the eleventh centuries, tea fell from favour at court and was no longer consumed.

In 1191, another Japanese monk, Yeisai-zenji, returned from China after studying Zen Buddhism there and brought with him not just more tea seeds but the new method of whisking powdered tea into hot water and the serving and drinking rituals developed by the Chinese Rinzai Zen Buddhist sect. Although that particular method of preparing powdered tea died away in China as steeped tea became fashionable, the Japanese adapted and developed it into a formalized and complicated ceremony. By the fifteenth century, the Japanese Tea Ceremony, *Cha-no-yu* (see page 86), was firmly established as an ideal tea-drinking event governed by precise rules. Three schools of tea were set up by the Zen Buddhist priests: Ikkyu, Shuko and Rikkyu.

Preparing for the elaborate Japanese tea ceremony.

Tea reaches Europe

We know that China was trading with Greece in the second century BC, and that the Han Dynasty was investigating the possibility of trading with the Roman Empire in the first century AD, but there is no mention of tea in records of the time. During the sixth and seventh centuries, the Arabs had a monopoly over trade between China and the West and there is still no record of tea having changed hands. Marco Polo arrived in China in 1271 but still no tea is mentioned.

Then, in 1559, Giambattista Ramusio, an Italian civil servant, wrote that a Persian traveller by the name of Hajji Mahommed had told him of *Chai Catai*, a herb used by the people of Szechwan Province in China to make a medicine for stomach-ache and gout. From that point on, we find several references that indicate a growing awareness of tea (though still no record that any actually arrived in a European port). The Portuguese set up a trading base on the Canton river in 1557 but shipped no tea. The Dutch, however, with their first trading base established at Bantam on the island of Java, sent their first cargo of China tea to Amsterdam in 1606. The Dutch people began to show an interest in this new herb in the 1630s, as indicated in a letter from the directors of the Dutch East India Company in 1637 to their Governor-general in Batavia: 'As tea begins to come into use with some of the people, we expect some jars of Chinese, as well as Japanese tea with each ship.'

In Holland, the newly imported tea was sold in apothecaries' shops and later in early grocery shops known as 'colonial warehouses'. The Dutch writer Jan Nieuhoff helped raise awareness of the herb at home and elsewhere after he met the Manchu rulers in Peking and experienced Chinese tea-drinking at first hand:

There is a great difference in the manner of preparing and using this liquor between the Chinese and those of Japan; for the Japanese beat the leaves into a powder and mingle it with boiling water in a cup which they afterwards drink off; but the Chinese put the leaves whole into a pot of boiling water, which having lain in steep for some time they sip it hot, without swallowing down any of the leaves, but only the Quintessence thereof extracted.

He also explained how the Manchus themselves prepared their tea:

They infuse half a handful of the herb Thea or Cha in fair water which they afterwards boil till a third part be consumed, to which they add warm milk about a fourth part, with a little salt, and then drink it as hot as they can well endure.

By the mid-1600s interest among the wealthy upper classes of Europe – for tea was a costly indulgence – was beginning to grow and so the Dutch began to re-export the tea they had shipped from China into Portugal, Germany and France. In France, in 1648, tea was referred to by a Parisian doctor as 'the impertinent novelty of the age'; the playwright Racine drank copious quantities; Cardinal Mazarin drank it as a cure for gout; and in 1684, in a letter to her daughter, Madame de Sévigné recommended that tea should be drunk with both milk and sugar. However, despite its favoured position in France as the most fashionable drink of the 1680s, tea quickly gave way to coffee, never to regain its early popularity.

In Germany, tea was at first drunk as a medicinal brew but, as in France, did not capture the long-term attention of the German people except in what is now called East-Frisia, in the northern part of the country, where tea has for more than 300 years been the chosen beverage. In Portugal, as in Holland, tea became a luxury beverage for members of the court and the wealthy upper classes, and it was here that Catherine of Braganza (see page 14), who was later to marry the English King Charles II, learned to love it. When she travelled to England in 1662 for her wedding she brought with her, as part of her dowry, ownership of the islands of Bombay and a casket of tea!

The first tea reached Russia in the early seventeenth century when the Mongolian ruler, Altyun-Khan, sent a gift of tea to Tsar Michael Fedorovich. Meanwhile, the signing of the Treaty of Nerchinska in 1689 marked the beginning of regular trade between the two countries. At first the drink was consumed only by the Russian elite but gradually other social groups discovered it and developed their own ways of brewing and serving the infusion. Until the late eighteenth century, supplies were transported to the Russian market by camels pulling caravans along the 'Great Tea Road' which ran from Kashgar behind China's Great Wall, through the Gobi Desert to Urga in Mongolia. At Usk Kayakhta, the teas were inspected and packed into paper and foil packages which were then stowed inside bamboo boxes, and loaded onto sledges and carts. From here, the laborious journey took between 16 and 18 months. It is said that 'Russian Caravan' tea acquired its slightly smoky flavour from the smouldering fires that kept the travellers warm at night during essential periods of rest and sleep. In fact, the black teas being transported to St Petersburg had acquired their slightly smoky character during manufacture, since the Chinese producers fired their drying ovens with freshly felled pine logs and the tea absorbed some of the sappy, smoky aroma that penetrated the drying room from the ovens below.

As demand for tea in Russia grew, quantities rose to more than 6,000 camel-loads a year. This made the transportation so expensive that traders were forced out of business, leaving a vacuum that was quickly filled by English and German merchants. In 1903, the opening of the Trans-Siberian railway made it possible to transport goods from China much more rapidly than by ship to London, Amsterdam or Lisbon, and oriental products now arrived in Moscow, Paris and Berlin in just over a week.

Tea for the British

An English collector of travellers' tales, by the name of Samuel Purchas, mentioned in 1625 in *Purchas His Pilgrimes* that the Chinese 'use much the powder of a certaine herbe called chia of which they put as much as a walnut shell may containe, into a dish of Porcelane, and drink it with hot water . . .'. In 1637, the Cornish traveller Peter Mundy wrote that the people of Fukien in China's Fujian Province 'gave us a certain Drinke called Chaa which is only water with a kind of herb boyled in it'.

So when Thomas Garraway started offering tea for sale at his general store in Exchange Alley in the City of London in 1657, it was not a totally unknown drink, but still Garraway recognized the need to advertise and, in 1660, wrote his famous broadsheet entitled *An Exact Description of the Growth, Quality and Vertes of the Leaf Tea.* In it he explained where tea came from, how it was produced and why it was good for you. Fourteen clauses claimed that tea would cure headaches, kidney problems, skin complaints, loss of memory, breathing difficulties, infections, drowsiness, insomnia, runny noses, watery eyes, aches and pains, fevers and colds, dropsy and scurvy. But tea, a rare oriental luxury, was expensive and made more so by a heavy tax imposed by the government, so Garraway's customers were at first few and far between and came occasionally from their aristocratic houses and palaces to buy half a pound or less at a time. With prices ranging from 16 to 60 shillings (equivalent to $1.50 to $5.90 a pound and average wages for servants such as butlers and footmen at £2 to £6

Catherine of Braganza, an early champion of tea in Europe.

Porcelain teapot that was used to serve tea to Queen Catherine at Ham House in the late seventeenth century.

their menfolk went off to the coffee houses to drink tea, coffee or chocolate (and various alcoholic beverages) with their professional colleagues and friends. Coffee houses had opened in the 1650s, first in Oxford and Cambridge and then in London, and served hot beverages and a range of beers, ales, ciders, wines, sherries, ports, possets and sherbets.

The first tea brought into London in the 1650s was not imported by an English company but by the Dutch East India Company, and it was not until 1669 that the English East India Company ordered its first cargo of 143 lbs. With the price of tea remaining high, demand was small, and when the Company shipped in large quantities, the result was a glut of tea on the London market. The high cost of tea continued into the eighteenth century, with the tax at 14 per cent on all tea imported by the East India Company plus an additional five shillings or so in the pound payable by the purchaser.

per year, it was only the Royal Family, wealthy members of the upper classes and highly paid civil servants who could afford such a commodity.

Catherine of Braganza inadvertently helped tea's cause when she arrived to marry English King Charles II in 1662. Coming as she did from Portugal, one of the first countries to import tea into Europe, Catherine had grown up drinking tea and was an avid fan. The precious tea inside the casket that she brought with her to England was brewed by her for her friends at court and so the new herb became a distinctly fashionable treat. Ladies drank their tea at home in their closets while

Because of its high cost, tea had, from its earliest arrival in England, developed close associations with stately homes, palaces, expensive furnishings, fine linens and tablewares, and stylish living. Upper-class families acquired fine porcelains, silverwares and expensive imported tea tables in order to display their good taste, status and wealth. Shelves in the closets of large country houses held porcelain tea jars imported from China, small earthenware and porcelain teapots and the little bowls and saucers used for drinking the brew.

At Ham House near Richmond in Surrey, the Duchess of Lauderdale ensured that she owned all the necessary tea equipage for those frequent visits from her friend Queen Catherine. A fine wooden tea table from Java had extra length added to its legs in order to make it the perfect height for tea. The closet contained a silver 'Indian furnace' for boiling the water and a lacquered box that held the tea and porcelain teapots and bowls. Despite the risk of burnt fingers, the Duchess sometimes served tea in unusual silver tea bowls.

Wall frieze of a tea party in the Chinese Room at Claydon House in Buckinghamshire.

At Saltram House in Devon, Chinese wallpaper showing the various stages of tea manufacture decorated the walls of the Chinese Chippendale Bedroom, while in other parts of this elegant Georgian house, cabinets and shelves held early examples of European and English pottery, as well as stoneware teapots and tea bowls, Chinese porcelain tea jars decorated with roses, and lidded tea bowls covered with butterflies and delicate oriental flowers.

As the wealthier classes bought more and more green and black leaf, and the poorer classes began to get a taste for the brew, black market traders developed a thriving system of smuggling and illicit distribution to meet the demand. Tea was much cheaper in Holland and France where taxation was lower, and entire communities in England (including priests, politicians and other upstanding members of the community) were involved in concealing, storing, buying and selling the illegal imports from those European countries. To benefit from high prices, unscrupulous merchants mixed the real leaf with the treated leaves of other plants and bushes, or purchased used leaves and dyed them back to the original colour using copperas (ferrous sulphate) and sheep's dung, molasses and clay, before drying and selling them on. The government attempted to stamp out such unacceptable practices by introducing fines of £100 for smugglers and traders of 'smouch'. Punishment became more severe in

Dr Samuel Johnson (1709–84), who declared himself 'a hardened and shameless tea drinker', taking tea in a Georgian English home.

1730 when the fine was increased to £10 per pound of tea. It was generally easier to produce polluted or 'fake' green tea, and a trend towards the safer black variety became evident – the start, perhaps, of Britain's preference for black leaf.

By the middle of the eighteenth century, tea had become the preferred drink of all classes in Britain. Ale and beer at breakfast had generally been replaced by tea; visitors to upper-class palaces, castles and manor houses were offered the brew; tea was served after the main meal of the day as a 'digestif to help settle the stomach' after copious amounts of rich food; tea provided refreshment in the workplace and paid part of the servants' wages; a cup was included with the entrance fee in the pleasure gardens of London; and it was available in inns and taverns for travellers. And while tea gradually became the drink of the British people, consumed in homes and workplaces across the land, the upper classes continued to brew and serve the beverage as an elegant refreshment in their stately homes. In the gardens of such homes, temples and follies that had once served as banqueting houses (where sweetmeats and desserts were served after dinner) now became the favourite venues for tea. Once the main meal was over, the assembled party would stroll through the gardens to the orangery, or tea-room, miniature castle, rustic cottage or 'temple', where tea was served. At Cliveden in Buckinghamshire, Lord

Orkney and his guests took tea in the Octagon temple, a two-storey building set on the edge of an escarpment overlooking the River Thames. Designed by the Venetian architect Giacomo Leoni, this charming building contained a small room (known as 'the grotto') on the lower level where tea equipage was stored, and an upper room, The Prospect Room, where guests drank tea and enjoyed the view. At Saltram House in Devon, 'The Castle' provided the perfect location for visitors to relax and take tea while admiring the beautifully landscaped gardens.

Until the early nineteenth century all the tea drunk in Britain was imported from China, carried exclusively on the ships of the English East India Company. But trade with China was becoming more and more expensive and problems were developing because of the trading of opium – an illegal but widely used drug in China. The East India Company was selling into China opium that had been grown on British territory in India, and in 1839 the exasperated Chinese emperor ordered 20,000 chests to be deposited on the beach so that it would be washed away by the tide.

In 1840, the British declared war on the Chinese and the Chinese retaliated by imposing an embargo on tea exports to Britain. Fortunately, by then, the tea plant had been found growing in north-eastern India, the first plantations had been established in Assam and the first British-grown Assam tea had reached the London tea auctions in 1839. During the 1850s, the gardens of Darjeeling were planted and cultivation spread up into Terai and Dooars in the 1860s. Trials were carried out in southern India in the 1830s but commercial production did not really get going there until the 1890s.

In Ceylon, now Sri Lanka, the first plantations were laid out in the late 1860s and by 1900 roughly 155,000 hectares (380,000 acres) of land were given over to tea. With more and more British-grown tea and less and less being imported from China, prices began to drop and tea truly became the everyday drink of the British people.

Before the production of tea in India and Ceylon made tea more readily available and increased British consumption, the speedy clipper ships of the 1840s, '50s and early '60s had played their part in the tea story by dramatically reducing the journey time from the Chinese ports. The name was first used in the mid-1840s to describe American vessels and probably derives from the equestrian term 'to go at a good clip'. Initially 'clipper' referred to almost any vessel that sped across water at an unusually fast pace, but gradually people started talking of coffee clippers, Californian clippers, tea clippers and China clippers.

These sleek, elegant ships were built for speed and, while traditional cargo ships sailed at less than five knots, clippers achieved up to 18 knots. In 1845, the American clipper

Baltimore completed the round trip from New York to China in just eight months. The British soon recognized the need to build their own clippers to compete and the *Stornoway* was launched from Aberdeen in 1850. The race for time and the promised high prices for the first teas home meant that competition between the clippers built to an annual frenzy. Brokers would camp out in the London docks ready to taste and bid for the best of the new arrivals. In 1866, in the most famous race of all, 40 vessels took part. Three ships, the *Taeping*, the *Ariel* and the *Serica*, sailed almost dead level right across the Indian Ocean and, 99 days after setting sail from the Canton river, the *Taeping* and the *Ariel* docked within 20 minutes of each other, with the Serica coming in just a few hours later. In 1871 the last of the clipper races thrilled the British public, by which time the Suez Canal had opened and steamships were carrying goods more quickly by that route.

Although by the beginning of the nineteenth century people across Britain were consuming growing quantities of tea, there was still no formalized 'afternoon tea' as we now know it. The credit for 'inventing' this now famous institution is often given to Anna Maria, 7th Duchess of Bedford, in the 1840s, but in fact she did not create a new meal, but merely renamed a social occasion that was already evolving because of changing mealtimes. In the seventeenth century, dinner was served at midday and lasted for four

IMMENSE SAVING
realised by all who use these delicious Teas

SUPPLIED FIRST HAND, DIRECT FROM THE GROWERS.
Delivered to any Address, Carriage Paid.

1/-, 1/3, 1/6, 1/9, & 2/- a lb.

Any Quantity can be had; but 7, 10, 11, or 20 lb. are packed in Canisters, 40, 65, or 100 lb. in Chests, without extra charge.

Write for Samples, forwarded Free of Charge, or, better still, send TRIAL ORDER, and you will be AMAZED at the Delicious Quality and Splendid Value.

"These Teas yield the BEST RESULTS. They are genuine and carefully prepared."—*Lancet.*

"Invalids may enjoy drinking these PURE TEAS without the least fear of any injurious effects."—*Health.*

Supplied to H.R.H. the Prince of Wales, H.R.H. the Duke of Connaught, and to Millions of Homes from the Palace of Royalty to the Peasant's Cottage.

Offices: 21, MINCING LANE, LONDON.

By the 1880s tea was grown on British soil in India and Ceylon, which forced the price of tea down low enough for everyone to drink more tea.

or five hours. This was followed by tea-drinking, accompanied by thinly sliced bread and butter, in the withdrawing room. As the years passed, the dinner hour grew later and later until, in the 1820s and 1830s, it was served at 7.30, 8 or even 8.30 pm. With breakfast at 9 or 9.30 am, and only a very light meal at midday in the form of the newly invented luncheon (also called 'nuncheon' or 'noonshine'), there was a long gap until dinner with no refreshment or sustenance. And so the Duchess and others like her called for their tea equipage in order to brew a private cup of tea in the boudoir or drawing room. Once

Anna Maria had made the idea fashionable by inviting her aristocratic friends to join her for a cup of 'afternoon tea', such social gatherings became an essential part of British life amongst upper-, middle- and working-class ladies. By the late 1860s, cookery books and manuals of household management were giving detailed instructions on how to organize a tea party, what foods to serve, the duties of the servants, where to place the furniture, what to wear, what entertainment to arrange, how to set out the tray, where to stand to receive guests, and at what time the guests should arrive and depart.

Tea, always regarded as a very 'respectable' drink in England, allowed ladies to entertain without risk of gossip.

At stately homes and country mansions throughout the land, tea parties became a regular occurrence and were often devised around a particular occasion – a birthday, a wedding, a fashionable sporting event, or perhaps a royal visit. At Waddesdon Manor in Buckinghamshire, the Rothschild family entertained the Prince and Princess of Wales to tea in the garden. A striped marquee was erected for the occasion and sat majestically on the lawn in front of the elegant towers of the house while the royal visitors relaxed in cane chairs and sipped their afternoon tea from fine bone china cups. In grand houses all over the country, China closets held several different tea sets in various designs with enough plates, cups and saucers to serve tea to at least 12 guests. At Tatton Park in Cheshire, the numerous tea sets included a 900-piece service in glass. An 1871 household inventory from Dyrham Park near Bath details a pink and white service, a blue and gold service, a white service, a tea service with a 'sprig pattern' and a service with a pink border, showing just how important tea just had become in the life of the country house.

In contrast to the elegance and refinement of 'afternoon tea', the Industrial Revolution had led to the development of a working-class evening meal called 'high tea', a robust and satisfying spread of hearty foods, accompanied by a pot of strong tea, served at 5.30 or 6 pm and designed to welcome workers home from their long shifts in factories, mines, workshops and offices. Whereas the point of afternoon tea was to gossip and chat, show off the latest fashions and sip tea, the point of high tea was to replace all the calories that had been burned up during a 10- or 12-hour shift of hard manual work. And while afternoon tea was and still is served in the drawing room or garden, with guests seated in low armchairs and sofas, high tea is served in the kitchen or dining room, with the family seated in high-backed chairs around the table.

Taking tea had been a popular part of the entertainment provided in the pleasure gardens of eighteenth-century London, but with the expansion of the suburbs and the building of new roads and houses, the gardens gradually closed. By the time 'afternoon tea' had become a part of British social life, there was nowhere to go 'out to tea'. That all changed in the 1870s and '80s when tea-rooms started to appear, first in Glasgow and then in London and other provincial towns. Stuart Cranston and his sister Kate were pioneers in Scotland, while in London the Aerated Bread Company (ABC) served the first cups

of tea in 1884 at the London Bridge branch of their bread and cake company. Other companies quickly set up their own successful tea-rooms in town while in rural Britain cottage gardens were converted into tea gardens where local farmers' wives and country ladies and their daughters would scurry to and fro with pots of tea, scones, biscuits and home-made cakes to satisfy the hunger and thirst of day-trippers, cyclists and walkers.

As tea became more and more popular, new tea trading companies were established all around Britain, allowing successful entrepreneurs to make small fortunes from their dealings in tea and other groceries. Julius Drewe founded the once-famous Home and Colonial Stores in 1885 and made tea the most important of the shops' products, with high-quality Indian teas at the top of the list. Within four years, Drewe owned 43 branches across Britain and managed to amass a fortune that allowed him to build Castle Drogo in Devon (designed by Sir Edwin Lutyens) and retire at the age of 33 to live the life of a country gentleman.

When the Edwardian period brought a new fashion for travelling and stylish living, luxury hotels offered comfort and refinement like never before. All had a tea lounge or palm court where every day at four o'clock tea would be served to the accompanying strains of a string quartet or palm court trio. During this period, tea-time took an eccentric turn by incorporating dancing into the afternoon event. Afternoon tea at home had often included musical entertainment and sometimes 'dancing on the carpet' but when the tango arrived in 1910 from Argentina, it shocked and thrilled everyone with its risqué steps and erotic style. By 1913 there were tango clubs and classes throughout London and people were flocking to tango tea dances in hotels, theatres and restaurants.

Changes in social patterns, due mainly to two world wars and the introduction in the 1950s of American-style fast-food restaurants and coffee bars, meant that tea-rooms gradually disappeared from the high street. Although the British did not stop drinking tea at home, the earlier fashion for going out to tea, tea dances and tea parties had gradually declined and tea began to play a less prominent role in the nation's social life. With the demise of so many tea-rooms, catering outlets seemed to forget how to serve good tea. Then, in the early 1980s, there began a gradual reawakening of interest in tea, with new tea shops opening, new books published, tea dances in London hotels attracting eager guests on Saturday and Sunday afternoons, and a realization that some of us were actually rather tired of self-service, fast-food outlets, plastic table-tops, greasy food and badly brewed tea. Since then, many new tea-rooms

have opened around Britain and hotels have improved their afternoon tea service. Instead of teabags, caterers are realizing that they must choose quality loose-leaf tea, brew and serve the tea well, make tea foods more exciting and appetizing by introducing flavoured breads for the sandwiches, light, home-made scones, exquisite pastries and cakes, and sometimes little extra treats such as mini crème brûlées or sorbets or, in summer, dishes of strawberries and cream. And for those who wish to brew good tea at home, new retailers have made quality loose-leaf teas more readily available in the high street, supermarkets have increased their range of teas, and the internet now brings us mail order teas at the click of the mouse. With increased coverage in the press and a growing interest in quality and choice, tea is once again attracting the attention it deserves.

Masons teapot, made in Staffordshire, England 1810–30.

Tea in North America

As migrant groups for Europe set sail for the new continent in the late seventeenth and eighteenth centuries, they carried with them their most vital and prized household objects, including their tea things. In 1650, Peter Stuyvesant brought the first tea to the Dutch in their newly established colony, New Amsterdam, and when the British took control of the city in 1674 and renamed it New York, they found that tea-drinking was already firmly established and as important there as in Europe. Good-quality drinking water was not readily available in the city and so special water pumps were installed. Coffee houses and tea gardens became popular gathering places, just as in England, with New York boasting its own 'Vauxhall Gardens', or 'Ranelagh'.

In the different regions of the new colonies, settlers drank tea according to their individual lifestyles. In elegant homes, tea was brewed in porcelain teapots and drunk from fine European cups and saucers, while country folk boiled their kettles on the open fire of the kitchen range and measured the loose leaf into humble pottery teapots. In 1670, residents of Boston became aware of tea but the trade there was not established until the 1690s. By the 1720s and 1730s, it had become a fashionable and popular drink and both Boston and Philadelphia acquired reputations for fancy tea parties and perfect tea-time manners, with tea-drinking closely associated with good breeding and social status. Tea was still expensive and very much an upper-class luxury. As in England,

wealthy households boasted fine porcelains imported from China, silverware fashioned by European and American silversmiths, fancy lace cloths and little silver teaspoons, pretty dishes for bread and butter and tea tables upon which to arrange the necessary tablewares.

The wealthy cities of New York, Boston and Philadelphia became centres for the trade, and tea and tea equipage now featured prominently on lists of items traded from Britain to the American colony. But because tea was so heavily taxed by Britain at the time, it was smuggled into other ports from Europe by independent merchants and the British government lost as much revenue here because of black market trading as it was losing at home. Total consumption in the colony was over a million pounds of tea each year, but only a quarter of this was actually traded from London. The rest was smuggled. In 1767, a temporary solution was found whereby London merchants could claim a refund of taxes if tea was re-exported to America. Prices fell and over half a million pounds of tea were 'officially' shipped into American ports. The following year, the amount rose further to 900,000 pounds.

The success was short-lived. After the high costs of the war against the French and the Native Americans that gave Britain control of the colony, the British government was eager to raise funds and proposed a tax on British goods imported into America. This resulted in a boycott of British goods and general unrest, and when a further direct tax of three pence in the pound was subsequently imposed on tea to raise money for the upkeep of British soldiers and civil servants stationed in the colony, the colonialists were inflamed. Since the British East India Company still held a monopoly on the trade of tea into America, there was no way to avoid the tax, and tea exports from Britain to America fell dramatically to just 226,156 pounds in 1769 and 108,629 pounds in 1770, while smuggling once again increased.

In February 1773, the directors of the East India Company sought permission from the government to ship some of its by now surplus stock to America and, with amazing lack of foresight, the Tea Act was passed that allowed the Company to send four ships, carrying a total of more than 100,000 pounds of tea, across the Atlantic. The rest is history. In New York and Philadelphia, shipments of tea were forced to turn back. In Charleston, customs officials seized the cargo. In Boston, when the *Dartmouth* arrived carrying 114 chests of tea, she tied up at Griffin's Wharf, the tea was entered at customs and the ship then lay in Boston Harbour for three weeks while unrest among the locals grew. Eight days later the *Eleanor* sailed into port and the *Beaver* tied up on 15 December. Enough was enough! On the night of 16 December 1773, to cries of 'Boston harbor a teapot tonight' and 'The Mohawks are coming', the three ships were boarded by a band of men disguised as Native Americans and for the following three hours 340 chests of

tea were split open with hatchets and the tea hurled overboard into Boston harbour. The British closed the port and sent troops in to occupy the city. And so it was that a major error of judgement over The Tea Act of 1773 led to the American War of Independence and the ultimate loss to the British crown of the American colonies.

Following Boston, exhortations were issued to all Americans to 'Throw aside your Bohea and your Green Hyson tea, And all things with a new-fangled duty', and the ladies of Boston declared that they had bid:

Farewell the Tea-board with your gaudy attire,
Ye cups and ye saucers that I did admire;
To my cream pots and tongs I now bid adieu
The pleasure's all fled that I once found in you . . .

However, tea did not disappear from American homes altogether. Direct trade with China was established in 1784 and George Washington, first President of the United States of America and an avid tea-drinker, gave instructions during the War of Independence which ensured that all officers and men received a regular supply of tea. He continued to serve his favourite beverage to guests at his home at Mount Vernon.

In the early part of the nineteenth century, the introduction of faster American sailing ships by the newly established American tea merchants, together with the 'clippers' of the 1840s, made transportation of tea from China to the United States much faster and allowed the American traders to cut deeply into Britain's markets.

By the turn of the twentieth century, America was confident and strong enough economically to hold the St Louis World's Fair in 1904. Traders and merchants from all over the world exhibited and it was here that Richard Blechynden, an English tea-planter, popularized iced tea. It was probably down to Blechynden that iced tea is as important to Americans today as hot tea has always been to the British. His original plan to offer samples of hot Indian tea to the visiting public was thwarted by exceptionally hot weather and so he served what he had brewed in glasses packed with plenty of ice. Iced tea and iced tea punches had actually been included in cookery books since the 1830s, after the invention of ice boxes, but Blechynden brought them to the notice of the general public and made them more widely popular.

A few years later, in 1908, another American tea merchant was responsible for inadvertently inventing the teabag. New York dealer Thomas Sullivan devised a stylish hand-sewn silk bag in which to send out samples of his teas to customers and they, finding the little bag very efficient and useful in a neat and tidy brewing operation, immediately demanded more of the same.

In the 1920s, prohibition, the motor car and the new independence enjoyed by women in the United States led to the opening of hundreds of new restaurants and tea-rooms right across the country. Tea-rooms with such names as The Blue Parrot Inn, Pine Tree Tea Room, Lady Baltimore Tea Room, Samovar, My Tea Wagon, Polly's Patio, The Cheshire Cat and many more sprang up in town centres, roadside resorts, village gardens, and in the lounges of hotels, inns and taverns – established and managed by women from all walks of life and from different backgrounds. Many bore scant resemblance to the stereotypical flowery parlours where little grey-haired old ladies nibbled on seed cakes and shortbreads. Some were bohemian garrets owned and staffed by artistic female entrepreneurs, some the stylish creations of adventurous, college-educated young women who favoured the modern look of the Arts & Crafts movement, some genteel and elegant establishments patronized by members of the upper classes, while others owed their success and charm to their Russian, Chinese, countryside, nursery rhyme or colonial theme. Sadly, just as happened in Britain, the fast-food boom of the 1950s led to the demise of the tea-room and by 1973 the *New York Times* was reporting that 'Ladies' tearooms are a dying breed'. Coffee bars and convenience food stores were starting to take over.

Tea continued to be available generally to American consumers but most hotels, catering outlets, fast-food chains and restaurants offered very poor quality, badly brewed and poorly served tea. Today, as the result of a resurgence of interest that started on the East and West coasts but is now spreading throughout the United States, many discerning American consumers are demanding better quality tea, properly served.

The renaissance of tea

In China and Taiwan, tea companies have recognized the growing market around the world for tea and have gradually opened up their industry to an increasing number of visitors and customers. And just as Europeans are now drinking more green teas, consumers in Asian countries have recently developed a taste for flavoured black teas, and so new tea shops and tearooms now offer a wide range of speciality flavoured varieties such as 'sticky toffee pudding', whisky, mango and mixed fruit flavoured teas.

In Japan, the exacting rituals of the traditional Green Tea Ceremony (see pages 86 and 243) are still taught in evening classes around the country. For many Japanese, the ceremony is an important part of social etiquette and it remains an accepted and highly respected part of Japanese culture. The ceremony is regularly performed at special events and for foreign visitors. The everyday tea for most Japanese is green Sencha or Bancha, or roasted Houjicha. In the past ten to fifteen years, however, a growing taste for black tea drunk with milk in the British style has led to the general availability of black teas in supermarkets and department stores and the opening of many English-style tea-rooms where little sandwiches are carefully prepared with their crusts cut off, and scones are served with clotted cream and home-made preserves. Tea has been the central theme for several major Japanese events and trade fairs during the past ten years and many Japanese ladies are keen to learn more of the history and ceremony of tea-drinking in Britain.

In the United States a growing interest – and in some areas a real passion – for tea is being fuelled by the opening of excellent tea-rooms, the wider availability of good-quality teas, an understanding of tea's health benefits, and a genuine enjoyment of the countless different flavours and strengths that tea offers. What makes this new passion for tea so fascinating and rewarding is the way in which those involved are creating something new by adding their own twist to the story. No longer is every tea-room in the United States a nostalgic Victorian replica of what may once have existed in Britain. Instead, tea-rooms and tea retail shops are inspired and influenced by a fusion of European, Asian, Oriental and American tea styles. The selection of teas, the teawares used and sold, and the foods offered on the menu reflect the same awareness of the many different possibilities. Some tea-rooms are now attracting much younger customers who meet to exchange ideas, do homework, drink tea and relax, and many shops and tea venues also organize regular tastings and talks that help customers understand what tea is, where it is grown, how it is produced, why teas vary so much, different brewing methods, its health benefits and much more.

Tea has also become the focus for education, medical and psychiatric specialists who are working with 'at risk' students at school, victims of

In keeping with the trend of offering tea advice to guests, the Blackberry Farm in Tennessee has a 'tea sommellier'.

of dedicated tea professionals.

In the UK, a small niche market for connoisseur teas is growing and a wider variety of teas is now on offer. The UK's Tea Council's annual competitions to find Top Tea Place and Top London Afternoon Tea have also helped push up standards. Tea-rooms are busier than ever and their customers are showing a much greater interest in, and also becoming more discerning of speciality single-source teas. As in the United States, an increased enthusiasm amongst the consuming public means a growing demand for a greater variety of teas, of higher quality, and for better standards of service. And as younger people begin to see tea as a stylish, healthy drink, tea is starting to take on more unusual guises – served in noodle bars that offer rare Chinese teas, in minimalist tea bars that offer quality brewed tea to take away as well as to drink on the premises, and in restaurants that offer a range of quality teas as an after-dinner alternative to coffee.

In many other parts of the world, people are discovering the benefits of tea and are seeking out information

crime, psychologically damaged patients and sick children. It seems that tea and its rituals help to create an atmosphere in which people feel safe, calm, nurtured and protected and in which they can discuss their experiences and feelings in a way that is not possible for them elsewhere. This enthusiastic and powerful movement is being supported and encouraged by regular conferences, trade exhibitions, training courses, group trips to India, Sri Lanka, China and Taiwan, set up and run by a very well-organized and focused network and suppliers as never before. In France, there are now more high-quality, elegant tea-rooms and tea salons than anywhere else in Europe and, as Glasgow was described in the 1880s as a veritable 'Tokyo of tearooms', so Paris is modern Europe's centre for tea. In Italy, health journalists, hoteliers, restaurateurs, event and wedding organizers, as well as tea-room owners and tea retailers, meet regularly to taste new teas, and to learn more about production, manufacture, brewing, serving and cooking with tea. In Germany, Spain, Holland, Belgium, Denmark, Sweden and Norway, and several countries of Eastern Europe, interest is also growing and retailers who have in the past sold modest amounts of tea are now finding that sales are increasing. In Moscow, five-star hotels are serving British-style 'afternoon tea'; in Georgia, tea-growers are exploring the possibility of opening a tea-room in Tbilisi to sell their hand-made teas and other quality teas from around the world; while in Hungary new tea retail stores are beginning to appear in malls and quality shopping areas. In India, tea bars are competing with the recently opened coffee chains and in Sri Lanka, some five-star hotels now offer guests the chance to drink speciality world teas in a stylish tea bar or tea room. And, with the enlargement of the European Union and a greater stability and financial growth in Eastern Europe, sales in such countries as Poland, Latvia and Lithuania are also growing.

Across the globe there is great excitement that the world of tea can offer such variety and choice: rich, strong, black teas from Africa and Sri Lanka; warm, smooth, malty teas from Assam; sappy first and second flush teas from Darjeeling; herby greens from Japan; sweet, velvety greens from China; rare, handmade teas from China and Taiwan; white teas with their silvery appearance and delicate fragrance; Puerh teas with their slightly earthy quality and accepted health benefits; and flavoured teas of all types. Today, even people who once claimed not really to like tea are finding flavours to suit their palate.

So what is fuelling this renaissance? Three forces seem to be at work. Firstly, there is a genuine surprise at the number of options available and a realization that there is a tea to suit all tastes. Secondly, there is a widespread recognition that tea is a much healthier option than coffee, contains less caffeine and gives us many useful ingredients, such as polyphenols, which act as antioxidants to help protect our bodies from certain cancers and other degenerative age-related illnesses. It is also widely accepted today that tea offers an excellent alternative to harmful alcohol, pairs well with oriental foods, aids digestion, adds to essential daily fluid intake and, more importantly, refreshes and revives us. Thirdly, tea brings with it an amazing history, culture and spirituality that enriches the lives of all those who work with it, drink it and serve it to friends. Every tea-drinking nation has its own tea culture and rituals, all of which link back to the Zen origins of tea-drinking amongst Chinese and Japanese Buddhist priests. Through brewing and drinking, as through Zen, we can learn to focus on aspects of life that have real significance and importance – beautiful objects, carefully performed ceremonies that calm and centre us, harmonious communication with others, the sharing of memorable, peaceful moments, and the creation of quiet times away from the demanding pressures of everyday life.

Naming the drink

In English, it is *tea*, but once upon a time, it was *tee* or *tay*. In India it is *cha* or *chai*. How did the different words develop?

The form of the name that entered each language depended on the route by which tea was first traded into that country. When tea first travelled outside China to the Arab countries and Russia, the Mandarin word, *cha*, spread with the goods. In Persian, Japanese and Hindi, the word settled as *cha*, in Arabic, *shai*, in Tibetan, *ja*, in Turkish, *chay* and in Russian, *chai*.

When the Portuguese first started buying tea from the Chinese, they traded through the port of Macao where the Mandarin word for tea had become *ch'a* in the locally spoken Cantonese. But Dutch tea ships sailed in and out of the port of Amoy in China's Fujian Province and so used the local Amoy word *te*, pronounced '*tay*', and changed it to *thee*. As it was the Dutch who were mainly responsible for trading tea to other European countries and beyond, the oriental beverage became known as *tea* or *tee* in English; *thé* in French; *thee* in German; *te* in Italian, Spanish, Danish, Norwegian, Hungarian, and Malay; *tee* in Finnish; *tey* in Tamil; *thay* in Singhalese; and *Thea* to scientists.

tea production:
leaf grades, blends and brewing

The tea plant

The tea plant (*Thea sinensis*), classified by the famous Swedish botanist Linnaeus in 1753, is an evergreen plant of the Camellia genus and is also known as *Camellia sinensis*. That is sub-divided into two main subspecies known as *Camellia sinensis sinensis*, the variety that was originally found growing in China and *Camellia sinensis assamica*, the plant that grows as a native of India's north-eastern province of Assam. A third, subspecies *Camellia sinensis lasio-calyx*, the Cambodian variety is not generally used for commercial production.

The plant grows as an evergreen shrub or tree that produces delicate little flowers with five or seven white or creamy-white petals and bright sunshine-yellow stamens, and whose sharply serrated leaves are thick and shiny. The bitter-tasting fruit is the size of a hazelnut and contains one to three seeds.

The Chinese bush generally grows to a maximum height of 5m (15 ft) and has several closely clumped stems, but ancient tea trees exist in China that reach heights of over 30m (100 ft), the oldest still growing in the Xishuangbanna region of Yunnan Province. The *Camellia sinensis sinensis* does not mind cold climates and grows well in China, Tibet, Japan and other high tea-growing regions of the world such as Taiwan and the upper slopes of the Darjeeling plantations in India. The leaves grow to roughly 5cm (2in) in length and the bushes can go on producing good tea for up to 100 years.

The slopes of Ambootia, an organic tea estate in Darjeeling, India.

The *Camellia sinensis assamica* is a tree rather than a bush, growing with a central trunk and reaching heights of 14–18m (45–60 ft). If allowed to grow freely, the leaves can grow to between 15–35cm (6–14in) in length. The Assam variety loves hot and humid conditions and goes on producing for approximately 40 years. There are five main types of *Camellia sinensis assamica* – the hardy Burma and Manipuri varieties, the Lushai variety, a tender-leafed variety and a dark-leafed Assam type. All give a darker, fuller-flavoured tea than the Chinese bushes.

The Cambodian variety is also considered to be a tree rather than a bush and grows with a single trunk to heights of roughly 4.5m (15 ft). It is generally only used in creating hybrids.

Today tea bushes and trees are grown commercially in between 40 and 45 countries around the globe, predominantly in areas close to the equator where the tropical conditions suit the plant best. The most suitable climates offer temperatures ranging from 10–35°C (50–85°F), rainfall of between 200–230cm (80–90in) a year, and elevations of between 300 and 2,100m (1,000–7,000 ft) above sea level. The best plantations are at altitudes of between 1,200–1,800m (4,000–6,000ft), where mist and cloud help protect the plants from too much direct sunlight and cooler air allows the delicate new buds and leaves to develop and grow more slowly, thus giving more flavour. The term 'high-grown' refers to teas

cultivated above 1,200m (4,000ft), 'mid-grown' to teas grown between 600–1,200m (2,000–4,000ft), and 'low-grown' to those cultivated below 600m (2,000ft).

The plant's shallow root system lies only a metre or so below the surface and is therefore vulnerable to droughts and floods. Soil that is too dry or that drains too swiftly will cause the bush to quickly wilt and stop producing new leaf buds. Too much rain and the roots will be drowned. So good drainage and suitable acid soil (clay, peat and sand are all good) are essential to successful cultivation.

Korean tea pluckers gathering leaves from a tea tree that has been allowed to grow to its natural shape and height.

Cultivating the plant

Today, rather than growing new bushes from seed, planters produce new stock by vegetative propagation from cuttings and cloned leaves taken from suitable 'mother' plants. The parent bushes are carefully selected for their ability to grow vigorously, give a high yield, withstand the onslaught of pests, resist drought or flooding and produce high-quality leaf. Tea Research Centres all over the tea-growing world have been working intensively for over a decade to develop ways of evaluating potential clonal stock and selecting faster-growing, higher-yielding plants. This allows farmers to develop plantations more efficiently and significantly raise profit margins.

The young plants are carefully tended in the nursery for a period varying from six to 20 months, depending on the climate, and are then planted out into the tea garden in a space measuring 1–1.5sq m (11–16 sq ft). Planting follows the natural contours of the landscape and the land is sometimes specially terraced to help eliminate soil erosion. The new plants are left unplucked and unpruned for two years until they reach a height of roughly 1.5–2m (5–6ft). They are then regularly pruned to keep them to a height of just under a metre and the bushes are encouraged to spread sideways and fill across to the neighbouring bushes. The surface created is referred to as the 'plucking table' and the new leaves that appear on the top are ready to be

A wide flat garden of tea in the Brahmaputra valley of Assam, India.

The nimble fingers of an experienced plucker in Georgia, Eastern Europe.

included in the manufacture of tea after they have spent three years, at lower altitudes, and five, at high elevations. In areas where very hot, direct sunshine threatens the health and growth of the plants, shade trees are planted to offer some protection.

In areas where weather conditions remain constant throughout the year, such as Kenya, the plant goes on growing without rest, while in regions where the seasons change, such as north-eastern India and China, there is a dormant period during which the bushes do not grow. Plucking takes place as the bushes 'flush' and push out new leaf shoots. In hot, steady climates, the plants flush regularly, while in cooler, seasonal regions picking goes on from early spring to late autumn. In some seasonal areas (for example in Darjeeling), the first flush is considered to give the best, most fragrant teas. These teas develop slowly in the cooler spring sunshine and enjoy the concentrated essence of the bush after the winter dormancy. But in other parts of the world, for example in Assam, it is the second flush that wins prizes and fetches higher prices.

For the finest black and green teas, the pickers 'fine pluck' the new shoots by taking only the first two new leaves and one new bud. For some oolong teas, young shoots of one bud and three or four leaves are often gathered from the bushes. The delicate new shoots are grasped lightly between the tip of the thumb and the tip of the

Andy Friend in Hawaii, planting up imported tea seedlings ready for the new tea estates on Kauai Island.

middle finger and then carefully broken off with a quick downward movement. The tender young shoots are then thrown over the shoulder into baskets or bags carried on the pickers' backs. In Darjeeling, where the leaves are small, roughly 22,000 new shoots are needed to give just 1kg (2.2lb) of made tea whereas in Assam, where the leaves are bigger, roughly 10,000 shoots will produce 1kg of made tea.

Pickers start work early in the morning while the dew is still on the bushes so that they can get the youngest, most tender, new growth and meet the targets set by quantity requirements.

The alternative to fine plucking is medium and coarse plucking. These give a larger quantity and weight of leaf but a lower quality of tea. With medium plucking, three leaves and a bud are snapped off, while coarse plucking includes all shoots that have two leaves and a bud, three leaves and a bud and four leaves and a bud. The climate and location affect how often the bushes are plucked. In Kenya, the bushes push out new shoots throughout the year and are plucked every 7–14 days. In Sri Lanka, new shoots are gathered every seven days in wet weather and every 10 days in dry. As the pickers work through the field or plantation, they also break off any coarse leaf and dormant shoots and throw them to the ground.

In some parts of the world, labour is either too expensive or simply not available for tea-picking and bushes must be harvested mechanically. Over

In some parts of Assam, pluckers collect the leaf in bags suspended from their heads; in other areas, the leaf is carried in baskets carried on the women's backs or heads.

the past few years, researchers have developed shears (used to clip the tea shoots off in much the same way as hedge clippers) and hand-held machinery that is manoeuvred by two workers over the plucking table. Alternatively, pluckers use large tractor-like machines that trundle between the rows of bushes, cutting off any top growth, and there is now a hovercraft style harvester that allows one man to 'drive' the harvester over the top of the bushes. Because machines can never be as discerning as human pickers, machine-harvested tea inevitably contains stalk and older, coarser leaves as well as fresh growth. This method consequently results in a poorer-quality tea.

A mechanical harvester working its way through a tea field in Argentina.

Care of the bushes

Each plantation or field of bushes is regularly pruned to remove any dead wood, to encourage vigorous growth and to maintain the even and constant height of the plucking table. While pruning is taking place, plantation managers also take the opportunity of cleaning drains and cutting new drainage channels into the soil.

Weed control is a crucial part of plantation husbandry and represents the second highest cost in tea cultivation after plucking. Young tea plants are more sensitive to the activity of weeds than mature plants and so need more intensive care. In some cases, hand-weeding and the use of hoes, sickles and forks keep the plants free from the predatory growth of unwanted plants, but the most widespread and efficient form of control is through the carefully controlled application of relevant herbicides.

The most common diseases affecting tea bushes are various root diseases, which can kill the plants, cause them to produce discoloured leaf or lead to the development of

Pruning back the bushes in Anxhi province, China

fungal growth on the bushes; stem and branch diseases, which can kill off individual branches and cause the growth of fungus; leaf diseases, which can cause discoloration and spotting on the leaves; and a lack of certain minerals in the soil, which can cause bushes to produce distorted leaves, discoloured flush, buds that do not develop or that die off, or leaves that are brittle or drop prematurely. All of these are treated with specific chemical and mineral applications to the soil or by removing the affected bushes and infilling with new stock. The plants can equally be damaged by insects, mites and rodents and these are dealt with by pesticides and population control.

The soil is enriched naturally by the application of manure, compost and mulched material gathered during pruning.

Tea types and manufacture

Across the globe, more than 10,000 different teas are made from different varietals of *Camellia sinensis*. As with the production of wine, the character, colour and flavour of each tea when it is brewed and served are determined by a long list of variable factors – location of the plantation, altitude, climate, seasonal changes, the soil, the minerals it contains the way in which it drains, cultivation methods, plucking methods, how the leaf is processed, what happens to the leaf at the end of the manufacturing process and the way in which the tea is eventually brewed. Teas are classified by the process used to make them and, although the names of the different categories (white, yellow, green, oolong, black, puerh and compressed) often tell us about the colour and appearance of the dry leaf, it is the manufacturing method that decides the category. Levels of caffeine (in the past also known as theine) vary in different teas. This is thought to depend on the varietal of the bush, the age of the leaf when it is picked, its location on the stem, the length of oxidation time, the size of the tea leaves brewed, the quantity of leaf used to make the brew, and the length of the brewing time. New buds and young leaves have been found to contain higher levels of both caffeine and antioxidants.

White tea

White tea was originally named after the tiny white or silver hairs that cover the bud as it develops at the tip of each tea shoot. Originally only made in China from two varieties of the tea plant (*Shui Hsien* or Water Sprite, and *Da Bai* or Big White), white teas are now being produced in other parts of the world using other varietals. And, although some white teas are made from only the new leaf bud (gathered before it starts to unfurl), other white teas are made from the new bud and one or two young open leaves or just from the open leaves, so don't be surprised to find other white teas made in other countries that look quite different from *Yin Zhen* Silver Needles. With the bud-style white teas, the size of the buds can vary from sturdy buds that measure up to almost 2.5cm (1in) in length, to much smaller, thinner and more wiry buds. In the same way, the size of the open leaf variety depends on the bush varietal used.

Once the new buds and baby leaves have been carefully gathered, they are dried in the sun or in a warm, drying room. When brewed they give a very pale, champagne-coloured liquor that has a very light, soft, sweet, velvety flavour. The antioxidant levels are said to be higher than in other types of tea.

Yellow tea

Yellow teas are among China's rarest. Manufacture is very similar to that of green teas but there is an extra stage during which the leaf is exposed to gentle heat and allowed to mellow by a process of non-enzymatic fermentation. Traditionally, this is achieved by gently firing the leaf after it has been pan-fried to kill the enzymes. The warm leaf is wrapped in 'cow skin paper', an old type of paper that has a yellow appearance, and allowed to dry naturally inside the warmth of this parcel for a few hours. The pan-firing and wrapping is repeated until the tea reaches the required look, feel and aroma. Yellow teas are slightly more yellow-green in appearance than green teas and when infused, give a pale, yellowy-green liquor that has a delicate, honey-like sweetness and a fresh aftertaste.

Green tea

reen teas are generally described as 'unoxidized' teas and no chemical change occurs during their manufacture. Processing differs from country to country but the basic manufacture sometimes involves a short period of withering to allow some of the water content in the leaf to evaporate, then steaming or pan-firing, to de-enzyme the leaf. Next comes a series of rollings and firings to shape and dry the leaf. Sometimes, the leaf is alternately rolled or shaped by hand, giving each tea its own characteristic appearance – for example, the tiny pellets of Gunpowder, the curved eyebrow shape of *Chun Mee* (Precious

Sorting manufactured green tea by hand in China.

Eyebrows), or the tightly wound spirals of *Biluochun* (Green Snail Spring). After shaping, or sometimes as the shaping process is taking place, the teas are dried in wok-like pans, in closed ovens, on baskets or cloths set over charcoal fires or in tumble dryers. Methods of shaping and drying vary from country to country and region to region. In many parts of China, Korea and Vietnam, for example, the teas are hand-crafted, sometimes with the help of some simple machinery, and the skills involved in making the teas are passed on from one generation to the next. In other producing regions, the manufacturing process has been totally mechanized or automated. In Japan, for example, the entire process for most teas is entirely mechanized and the leaves are first steamed on a rapidly moving conveyor belt to make them soft and supple, then mechanically cooled and repeatedly rolled, pressed, sorted, polished and dried before being cooled again and packed at the end of the production line.

Freshly plucked leaves tumbling in a panning machine that de-enzymes them before shaping and drying them into green tea.

A steaming machine used to de-enzyme leaf during the manufacture of steamed green teas.

Oolong tea

Oolong teas, known as partially or semi-oxidized (or partially or semi-fermented) and sometimes referred to as 'blue' or 'blue-green' teas, are traditionally manufactured in China and Taiwan, but other countries are now also producing them.

Two very different methods of production are used to manufacture two different styles of oolong – dark, open-leafed oolongs and greener, balled oolongs. Darker, open-leafed oolongs are made by withering the leaf in the sun outdoors and then indoors on bamboo baskets. This allows some of the water in the leaf to evaporate and starts the oxidation process. The leaves are turned every two hours and shaken or 'rattled' in

Fresh leaf for oolong tea withering on bamboo baskets in a factory in Fujian province, China.

the baskets to break the cells inside and on the surface of the leaf. When the oxidation level has reached about 70%, the leaf is turned for 5–10 minutes inside a hot panning machine to halt any further oxidation and then dried in hot ovens. These darker oolongs can be infused several times, give a pale amber liquor and have a soft fruity, honeyed character with undertones of peach and apricot.

The manufacture of the greener, rolled or 'balled' oolongs starts with the withering and tumbling of the leaf as for the darker oolongs. When they have reached 30% oxidation, the leaves are put through the hot panning machine for 5–10 minutes to stop any further oxidation, then dried and allowed to rest overnight. Next day, the leaf is wrapped inside large cloths to form balls that contain 9 kg of tea. Each bag is tightened and then rolled in a special rolling machine to bruise and squeeze the leaves inside. The bag is then opened and the compacted leaf is separated and immediately wrapped into a ball again. This tying and rolling of the bags is repeated at least 36 times and sometimes up to 60 times until the leaves are tightly rolled up into rough green pellets. The semi-balled tea is then dried in large ovens. These greener oolongs can also be infused several times, give a very pale amber-green liquor and have a wonderful fragrant character that is often reminiscent of narcissus, hyacinth and lily of the valley.

Bao Zhong (Pouchong) teas are another type of oolong but because of a much shorter oxidation time, they are closer to green teas and have a much greener appearance.

Bamboo tumbling drum used to 'rattle' leaf for oolong tea prior to oxidation.

Black tea

Pluckers are paid according to the quantity of fresh leaf they pluck. At the end of each session, the leaf is carefully weighed and a record kept.

In China, these are defined as 'red teas' because of the coppery-red colour of the liquor that they yield. When the Chinese talk about 'black tea', they mean 'puerh' (see pages 47, 48, 138–45).

For black tea, methods of manufacture and the varieties produced vary enormously from country to country and from region to region, but the process always involves four basic stages – withering, rolling, oxidation (also misleadingly referred to within the tea industry as 'fermenting') and firing (drying). The two major processing methods are 'orthodox' and 'CTC'. The traditional orthodox method is still used in China, Taiwan, India, Sri Lanka, Indonesia and elsewhere, and tends to treat the leaf with more respect than the modern CTC method. For orthodox teas, the leaves are spread out in warm air and allowed to wither for up to 18 hours in order to reduce their water content (78–80 per cent when plucked, 55–70 per cent after withering). The leaves are then soft and pliable, ready for rolling. The yellow-green leaf is then put into in a special rolling machine that presses and twists the leaves, breaking the cells inside them and releasing the natural juices and chemicals that will start the oxidation process. After the first roll, the smaller pieces of leaf are sifted off and the larger particles

CTC machines that chop the leaf into tiny particles for tea bags.

Chopped leaf oxidising in troughs in a factory in Assam, India.

are put back into the roller for a second and sometimes third rolling. The leaf is also sometimes put through a rotorvane machine (a little like a large mincing machine that twists and breaks the leaf even more than the orthodox roller) to maximize production of smaller broken grades of leaf. After rolling, the leaf is broken up and spread out in thin layers in cool humid air and left to oxidize for 20–30 minutes or longer, depending on the conditions and temperature. The leaf now begins to develop its recognizable aroma and flavour, becomes darker in colour and develops the tea chemicals known as theaflavins and thearubigins. To arrest the oxidation, the tea is finally fed into large automatic dryers inside which it is carried along on conveyor belts or on a moving stream of hot air in temperatures of 115–120°C (240–250°F) and this reduces the moisture content of the tea to just 2 to 3 per cent. 'Fluid bed dryers' that blow the particles of tea on a stream of hot air are the most efficient type and

ensure that all the pieces of leaf are evenly dried.

The CTC (Cut, Tear and Curl) method of manufacture is widely used in major tea-producing countries to give a small-leafed tea that brews more quickly and yields a strong liquor – characteristics that are desirable for the production of teabag blends. This process was developed in the 1950s when the teabag was becoming more popular. To produce such teas, the leaf is withered in the same way as for orthodox teas but, instead of being rolled, it is macerated by the blades inside a CTC machine that rotate at different speeds, or in a Lawrie Tea Processor (LTP) rotating hammer-mill leaf disintegrator, which tears and breaks the leaf into tiny particles. The remaining oxidation and drying stages of the process are the same as for orthodox black teas. In modern factories, oxidation usually takes place on a conveyor belt that slowly moves the oxidizing tea towards the oven.

Puerh tea

uerh tea is called 'black tea' by the Chinese and was exclusive to China for centuries. Puerh tea is thought to have various positive health benefits and is consequently becoming more and more popular throughout the world. Named from the market town where the teas have been traded for hundreds of years, puerh teas have an earthy, mature character and are said to be excellent for the digestion, to ease stomach upsets, to help reduce cholesterol in the blood and to help those on a diet to lose weight more easily.

Traditionally, puerh teas come from Yunnan Province in south-west China and are made from a large-leafed variety of *Camellia sinensis* that grows in the area. The particular varietal of the tea bush, along with the Yunnan soil and the climate in the region produce teas that have a rich, woody, slightly earthy character and when the leaf is matured or aged by a special process in special conditions, it

Puerh tea drying in the sun during manufacture in Yunnan province, China.

acquires an elemental, slightly 'mouldy' character.

Puerh teas are classified into two types – 'raw puerh' (some people refer to this as green or semi-green puerh but these terms are not correct) and 'cooked puerh' (also sometimes known as finished or ripe puerh). Raw puerh is made by withering, pan-firing to kill the enzymes, rolling and kneading, then sun-drying for high quality leaf or air drying for less expensive teas. The leaf may then immediately be steamed and compressed into round cakes or flat rectangular slabs or it may be left loose. The tea is then allowed to mature for a year or more before being compressed. The maturation period allows a slow, natural fermentation in naturally warm and humid, well-ventilated conditions. Because of the water content in the tea and the oxygen in the air, the leaf slowly ferments (this really is fermentation and is different from the oxidation that takes place during the manufacture of black and oolong teas) and turns the leaf from green to red and then to dark brown. The loose or compressed teas are then aged for up to 50 years in conditions where humidity and temperature are carefully controlled to encourage the puerh to develop a mature, complex, earthy flavour and aroma. As the tea ages, the less astringent and bitter and the sweeter and smoother the flavour becomes.

The best of these raw puerhs sell for thousands of dollars ($8000/£4000) and are often now bought as investments.

The manufacture of cooked puerh was developed in the 1970s to replicate the mature earthiness of raw puerh by a faster method. The leaf is picked, withered and then mixed with a carefully measured quantity of water and a bacterial culture taken from ancient puerh. The tea is then piled and covered for up to 40 days in a hot, very humid room. From time to time the covers are removed in order to regulate the amount of heat and moisture that builds up in the piles of tea and the mixture is regularly turned to distribute the bacteria, the heat and the moisture evenly through the mass of leaf. The bacteriological activity causes the leaf to change from a yellowy-green to a reddy-brown. After this process of piling and fermenting, some maturation is necessary in order to allow the flavour of the fermentation to dissipate.

Cooked puerh at best offers a good mellow cup but without the complexity and sappiness of the fresh leaf.

When the discs or cakes of puerh are ready for sale, they are individually wrapped in tissue paper and then placed singly into presentation boxes or stacked in sevens and wrapped in bamboo leaves or grasses to protect the quality.

Compressed tea

More than one thousand years ago in China, during the days of the Tang Dynasty (AD 618–906), tea producers started compressing processed tea leaves into cakes or bricks in order to conserve the leaf and make it easier to transport. Many compressed teas that are available today actually consist of puerh tea, though others are made from normal black teas. The shapes of compressed teas vary from neat little bowls to flat circles or triangles, bowls shaped like birds' nests, globes in the form of a melon, tiny discs or balls and rectangular or square slabs. Some are wrapped in bamboo or dried banana leaves; others are packed inside grasses or paper. Some are packed singly, others in a stack of four or more cakes. To brew compressed teas, the required amount is flaked or broken off with the fingers or a knife blade and the crumbled tea is then steeped in hot water for one to five minutes. The longer the tea is steeped, the darker the colour of the liquor and the stronger the flavour.

Flavoured tea

Any type of tea – white, green, oolong, black or puerh – may be scented or flavoured with flowers, fruits, spices or herbs. The additional flavourings, in the form of flower petals, pollen heads, dried herbs, pieces of dried fruit or spice, are blended with the leaf at the end of the manufacturing process. Blenders also usually add flavouring oils or granules to the mixture in order to ensure an even, enduring flavour and aroma. Oils are generally used for loose blends and granules for teabag blends. Once flavoured, the teas are then packed as teabags or loose leaf.

One of the best known flavoured teas is Earl Grey, which is made by blending black, green, oolong or white tea with the essential oil of bergamot. This Chinese citrus fruit gives the tea a refreshing orange-lemon flavour. Other flavoured teas popular around the world are Jasmine, made by allowing the heady perfume of fresh jasmine flowers to permeate the tea; Rose Petal, which has the deliciously sweet scent of pink roses; and mint, which is usually made with China Gunpowder and pieces of dried mint leaf. The possibilities are endless and today's flavoured teas range from such simple mixtures as lemon tea to complex blends that include several different flowers and exotic spices.

Some teas have their own natural flavouring, acquired from the plants amongst which they grow. One particular variety of orchid tea from China, for example, absorbs the rich sweetness of the orchids that grow wild in the tea garden. And tea bushes that grow adjacent to fruit trees will naturally take on a hint of the scent given off by the blossoms and the fruit.

Flavoured teas should not be confused with herbal infusions that are made from plants other than *Camellia sinensis* (the tea plant). Many herbs and flowers, for example camomile, mint, rosehip and hibiscus, are used to give soothing, beneficial brews but if the leaves of the tea plant are not included, neither the dried product nor the liquor should be referred to as 'tea'. The correct name is 'infusion', 'herbal' or 'tisane'. Packaging should make it clear to consumers what is actually inside the packet – just tea, tea mixed with flavourings, or just herbs, flowers, spices and fruits.

Decaffeinated tea

It is the caffeine that gives tea its ability to refresh us, increase our ability to concentrate and keep us going through the day. Caffeine is a stimulant that helps increase the speed of our reactions, makes us more alert, stimulates the digestive system and the activity of the kidneys and so helps to clean the body of unwanted toxins. There is an important difference in the way in which we absorb the caffeine in coffee and the caffeine in tea. When we drink coffee, the caffeine content goes instantly into our circulatory system, jolting us into wakefulness, causing the pulse to beat faster and the blood to pump more vigorously around our bodies. When we drink tea, the caffeine is released much more slowly (because of the controlling effects of the other ingredients in the tea) and takes 15 to 20 minutes to be absorbed. So, instead of being released into the bloodstream, the caffeine goes more gently into our central nervous system and helps to heighten our senses and increase our wakefulness. The effects of the caffeine in tea are therefore felt more slowly, stay with us for longer and tail off more gradually than with coffee. Tea really is a much more efficient 'pick-me-up'.

Caffeine is a mild cardiac stimulant and a mild diuretic and can cause problems for people with heart or kidney conditions. For those who cannot or do not wish to take caffeine into their bodies, decaffeinated tea is readily available, although the quality and flavour vary considerably, depending on the decaffeination process. Three different methods are used to remove the caffeine – carbon dioxide, methylene chloride and ethyl acetate.

Carbon dioxide is an organic solvent that is cheap to use, easy to remove from the tea after decaffeination, and harmless in small quantities. CO_2 is pumped into a chamber containing tea and it bubbles through the tea solution to remove the caffeine. The CO_2 is then removed from the chamber, separated from the caffeine and reintroduced into the chamber to absorb more caffeine. This process is repeated several times. The benefits of this method are that no chemical residue is left in the tea and the flavour and tea compounds are relatively unharmed.

Methylene chloride is the most popular and most widely used agent to extract caffeine from tea and is easily removed from the tea after decaffeination. It is approved by the American food standards body, the FDA (the Food and Drug Administration section of the US Department of Health and Human Services).To decaffeinate tea, the methylene chloride is applied either directly or indirectly to the tea. During the 'direct' method, the methylene chloride is applied to wet tea leaves and then removed with the caffeine. The decaffeinated leaves are then washed and dried. During the 'indirect' method (whereby the methylene chloride never comes into contact with the tea itself), the tea is first soaked in water to extract the caffeine (and other tea ingredients such as polyphenols and oils that give the tea its flavour and health benefits). The caffeine and water are then mixed with methylene chloride and heated to evaporate the caffeine and methylene chloride, leaving water and tea extracts which are then reintroduced to the tea.

Ethyl acetate is classed as a natural element that is found in tea, coffee, wine and bananas and is used in flavour enhancers for ice-creams, confectionery, cakes and perfumes. Because it occurs naturally, some people consider it to be the best agent for decaffeination and the FDA considers it to be GRAS (Generally Regarded as Safe). However, during the decaffeination process, it extracts other components as well as the caffeine and is difficult to remove from the decaffeinated tea.

Organic tea

The cultivation of any food product under organic rules is extremely rigidly controlled by various international bodies. No chemical fertilizers, pesticides, herbicides or other chemical additives of any kind may be used anywhere on the plantation and producers must rely totally on natural methods of pest and insect control, and on sprays, mulches and fertilizers that are made from dung, natural compost and other organic matter. Companies involved in organic production are concerned with the long-term health of our planet and organic tea plantations try to give back to the earth as well as take out. By using natural pest control (for example by reintroducing ladybirds), they aim to protect rather than harm the environment while at the same time producing tea that is totally free of chemical additives. Organic production is labour intensive and therefore expensive but as more people around the globe begin to share the organic producers' concerns, an extensive range of organic tea products is becoming widely available through tea retailers and supermarkets.

Even without organic production methods, tea is actually an incredibly clean product whose cultivation and production are tightly controlled by strict EU and US rules of health and public safety. Yet the number of people who take into consideration the long-term health and viability of the planet when buying everyday commodities, and who care about and appreciate the fine quality and flavour of organic products, is now considerable, and continues to grow. For them, a wide range of organic teas is now available from Africa, Sri Lanka, India, China, Japan and elsewhere.

Yarrow is one of several herbs grown at Ambootia, an organic tea estate in Darjeeling, for homeopathic-type soil preparations.

Bio-dynamic tea

Cow horns used for bio-dynamic soil preparations at Ambootia, an organic tea estate in Darjeeling.

S ome planters have taken organic production one step further and work in harmony with the universe to produce what is called 'bio-dynamic' tea. This means that the seasons, the weather, the waxing and waning of the moon and the interaction and interdependency of different species of insects, birds and animals are all taken into consideration when planting, pruning and all the other aspects of tea cultivation are being planned and implemented. Methods are based on the teachings of Rudolf Steiner and include the use of worm culture (vermiculture) to create large quantities of organic compost from grass cuttings, green manure, dung and coconut waste, and natural feed for the tea bushes prepared from cow horns lost by first lactation cows and buried for six months with herbal matter such as yarrow, stinging nettles and camomile. This approach to tea farming links with ancient agricultural practices when crops were grown in close harmony with these natural cycles. Demeter International is one of the bodies that runs a biodynamic certification scheme and invests in raising awareness of ecological patterns and sustainable farming activities.

Instant tea

Although manufacturers have been working for a number of years to produce an instant tea that competes successfully with instant coffee, none of the products available offers a flavour that resembles the true flavour of tea. Real tea connoisseurs consider instant tea to be an anathema and would never brew tea in this way. The idea of spooning a measure of dry granules or powder into a mug or cup and dissolving it in boiling water has nothing whatsoever to do with the brewing of a good cup of tea. The traditional brewing ceremonies in different cultures around the world – involving loose-leaf tea, a measuring spoon, a brewing vessel and beautiful cups or bowls from which to drink – are as much about the ritual as they are about preparing the drink and should never be abandoned for the sake of saving a few minutes. That time gained is time lost in terms of the calming influence and spiritual rewards of a traditional tea ritual.

Instant tea is manufactured by infusing tea leaves in water to extract flavour, caffeine and other tea components. The leaf and the brew are then separated, the leaf is discarded, and the solution is further treated to obtain a solid dry product. This is achieved by first heating the solution to evaporate the water content, then freezing the solution so that ice particles can be separated out, and finally filtering the solution through special membranes which hold back the solids but allow the water to pass through. After separation, the solids are freeze-dried or spray-dried and the resulting powder or granules are carefully packed in air-tight or vacuum packs. Whereas loose-leaf tea is rarely packed into glass jars, instant tea is almost always packed in this way.

Some companies are now producing instant teas flavoured with fruits and flowers, as has long been the practice with loose teas. Attempts are being made to create a finished product that is more attractive in terms of aroma, taste and colour, and packaging is beginning to reflect a more modern and stylish approach, in an effort to lure tea-drinkers away from traditionally brewed tea. A large proportion of the instant tea powders manufactured today are used in the production of ready-to-drink iced teas.

Ready-to-drink tea

For many years in Japan, 'ready-to-drink' (RTD) teas have been available from machines on street corners and in supermarkets. The range offers hot or cold, green or black, with milk or without, sweetened or without sugar, tea from Japan or from Darjeeling and Assam. It is very common to see people feeding coins into one of these machines in order to obtain the right tea for the occasion or the weather.

The market for such RTD teas has been growing in the West since the early 1990s when the American tea industry launched the first bottled and canned, still and carbonated, tea-flavoured drinks. To capture the largest possible share of the market and to give new products the benefit of a major advertising drive, tea companies joined forces with soft drink and cola manufacturers to create a range of tea-based, fruit-flavoured convenience drinks. These were marketed through supermarkets, convenience stores and small retail shops in competition with colas and other similar drinks. Since then, many new varieties have appeared, some over-sweetened, some with no sugar at all, some based on black tea, others using Japanese and Chinese green tea extracts, some with herb, spice and fruit flavourings, some with nothing but the tea and water in the bottle. The amount of tea in any of these drinks is minimal but the best of the selection do offer a much more appealing and satisfying drink than some of the more familiar cold canned and bottled drinks that contain far too much sugar, are far too gassy and never seem to quench one's thirst.

Fair trade tea

By purchasing 'fairly traded' goods, consumers aim to help ensure that workers in producing countries are not exploited but receive a share in the profitability of the company they work for. Tea has always been a very ethical industry and workers in most countries are well paid (in relative terms, according to average pay in the country in which they live and work). Plantations are generally run as small communities where provision of good housing and water, crèches, schools, clinics and hospitals is a prime concern of the plantation owners. However, Fair Trade attempts to redress the imbalance between the wages of workers in the developing countries and the profits made by major companies in the consuming countries. Products are sold through the normal channels of supermarkets, smaller retail outlets, websites and mail order catalogues. A percentage of the profits is paid back to the producing estates and goes towards improving the quality of life for the workers through pension schemes, alternative training programmes, welfare and medical programmes, and to improving the environment through important initiatives such as the planting of trees to stop soil erosion and landslides. Fair Trade teas are now available from various approved sources in China, India, Sri Lanka, Nepal, Tanzania, Uganda, Zimbabwe, Kenya and Vietnam.

The Ethical Tea Partnership

In the UK, the Ethical Tea Partnership, set up in 1997 under its original name of the Tea Sourcing Partnership by a group of British tea-packing companies, works with similar objectives to Fair Trade but in a different way. The ETP seeks to monitor conditions on tea estates in the countries from which British tea blenders and packers buy their teas – Argentina, Brazil, China, Kenya, Malawi, Sri Lanka, India, Indonesia, Tanzania and Zimbabwe – because its members believe that they have a shared responsibility for the social and ethical conditions involved in tea production, packing and supply. The organization seeks to guarantee that member companies only buy their tea from ethical producers who comply with local legislation and union agreements concerning terms and conditions of employment, health and safety, maternity and housing on the estates, as well as education and basic rights.

Whereas prior to 2008, monitoring was based on local legislation, ETP has since expanded its global standard and this is now based on the Ethical Trading Initiative's base code principles, environment and community issues which are enriched by trade union agreements and country laws. Greater focus is now placed on establishing best practice in tea estates and factories and on the estate management systems that are aimed at upholding ETP standards. ETP members have the option of placing the ETP logo on the front of their packs with the strap line "working for a responsible tea industry".

What's in tea?

The leaves of *Camellia sinensis* contain a number of chemicals (including amino-acids, carbohydrates, mineral ions, caffeine and polyphenolic compounds) that give tea its characteristic colour and flavour. They also contain 75–80 per cent water, which is reduced, during the first withering stages, to 60–70 per cent. The firing or drying process deactivates the enzyme that causes oxidation and reduces the water content to approximately 3 per cent.

During oxidation, polyphenolic flavanols (or catechins) react with oxygen to create the unique flavour and colour of the infused liquor.

The aroma of tea is extremely complex and so far more than 550 chemicals have been identified in the aroma of black tea. These include hydrocarbons, alcohols and acids, most of which are formed during the manufacturing process and which add their own qualities to the flavour and aroma of the tea. However, the taste mainly results from the various polyphenolic compounds (often incorrectly called tannins) being modified by caffeine. Both black and green teas contain similar amounts of polyphenols (flavanoids), although quantities vary in different types of tea. Green tea contains simple

The tea plant Camellia sinensis *with its delicate white flowers and tough, evergreen leaves.*

flavanoids called catechins while oolong and black teas contain more complex flavanoids called theaflavins and thearubigins. These flavanoids act as antioxidants in the body and help work against the effects of 'free radicals', which are formed in our bodies as a result of many forms of pollution and are thought to cause age-related diseases, such as heart disease, and cancer. Interestingly, evidence from tests recently carried out on 35 different teas suggests that polyphenols are present in higher quantities the higher the altitude at which the teas are grown.

Tea also contains theanine, an amino-acid that occurs rarely in nature and is thought to reduce physical and mental stress and promote a sense of well-being and relaxation. It is the magic ingredient that gives tea its famous reputation as the drink that calms you when you are anxious and agitated and stimulates you when you are sluggish or low in energy.

The caffeine content of tea acts as a mild stimulant and helps increase the activity of the digestive system and the kidneys, as well as raising general alertness, improving performance and combating tiredness. All types of tea contain caffeine but the amount of caffeine in each cup of tea varies according to the bush varietal, the age of the leaf or bud when picked, the amount of tea brewed and the number of minutes the leaves are allowed to steep. Some new buds and young leaves have been found to contain more caffeine than older leaves. In general, a cup of tea contains between a third and a half of the caffeine in a cup of coffee. Those people who do not wish to take caffeine into their bodies should therefore choose a herbal or fruit infusion which contains no caffeine at all.

Tea also contains traces of calcium, zinc, potassium, manganese, Vitamins B1, B2, B6 and B12, folate, niacin, and pantothenate. Although tannins are present in tea, this does not mean that tea contains tannic acid, as is often assumed. Tea tannins are astringent plant polyphenols that give a bitter or astringent flavour when tea is brewed.

Tea and health

When tea was first drunk in Ancient China, it was considered to possess health-promoting properties and, as well as being drunk after meals as an aid to digestion, it was used in ointments and skin creams. When tea arrived in Europe, it was sold by apothecaries and advertised as a tonic brew that had the power to cure stomach complaints, skin disorders, headaches, fevers, loss of memory, sleepiness and many other everyday ailments.

Until the twentieth century, few of the health claims made on behalf of tea had been proved, but recent research around the world and co-ordinated studies have given us more and more evidence that tea does indeed have many tangible health benefits. We now know that tea contains polyphenols that have an antioxidant effect in the body and

The UK Tea Council's logo used to promote the health benefits of tea drinking.

can help protect us against certain age-related and degenerative diseases. These antioxidant effects have been compared to those of certain fruits and vegetables: one study concluded that drinking three cups of tea a day was equivalent to eating six apples. In the case of heart disease and stroke, reports indicate that tea can help reduce the inflammation connected with atherosclerosis and vascular problems. Tea polyphenols have also been shown to inhibit the development of cancer cells. Studies with animals have revealed that tea flavonoids may help protect against skin cancer, lung cancer and digestive cancer in mice and rats.

Studies in a number of different countries indicate that tea is also helpful in reducing blood cholesterol, and it is thought that puerh and oolong teas are particularly beneficial.

Tea also aids good dental health, as the polyphenolic components in tea have the effect of helping to reduce the formation of plaque and bacteria in the mouth while the fluoride content strengthens tooth enamel and helps reduce the development of cavities. Green tea contains twice as much fluoride as black. In China and Japan toothpaste is now made containing a certain amount of tea extract.

Leaf grades

When tea emerges from drying machines at the end of the manufacturing process, it consists of a mixture of different-sized pieces of leaf. For successful brewing, these pieces must be sorted into different grades (or sizes), since different-sized particles brew at different rates. If the particles are of mixed sizes, the tea will brew unevenly. So, once the tea has been dried, it is either sorted by hand or passed through sifters with graduated mesh sizes to separate the particles. The different sizes are then classified according to size, type and appearance. Systems of classification vary from country to country.

In China, teas are named by region, the time of year when the tea was picked, the method of manufacture, the leaf type used, or the legend behind the origination of the tea. For example, *Chun Mee* means Precious Eyebrows, from the gently curved shape of the dried green leaves; *Jiuqu Wulong* means Nine-Bend Stream Black Dragon (*Jiuqu* means Nine-Bend Stream and *Wulong* or *Oolong* translates as Black Dragon); and *Rose Congou* is black tea skilfully made by hand (*Congou*, like *kung fu*, comes from the Chinese word *gongfu* and has to do with skill, as in Chinese martial arts), and blended with dried pink rose petals before packaging. Within each type of tea, grading is according to quality and uses words such as 'special' for the finest and 'common' for the lowest grade, with grades 1–7 in between. Oolong teas are classified by names such as 'choicest', 'finest fine' and 'extra fancy'.

In Taiwan, terms like 'fully superior', 'fine to finest', 'fully good' are used to grade oolongs while in Japan, green teas are described as 'good common', 'finest fine' and 'extra choicest'.

In India, Sri Lanka and other traditional producing countries where the orthodox method of manufacture for black teas is still used, grading terms divide the leaf into 'leaf' grades and 'broken' leaf grades. Broken leaf grades refer to what is left after the larger leaf grades have been sifted out.

In the African continent and in other countries that manufacture black tea for use in teabags by the CTC method (see page 46), a further system of grading terminology has developed in order to differentiate the much smaller grainy particles known as 'dusts' and 'fannings'.

Black Tea Category

Flowery Orange Pekoe (FOP)

This denotes tea made from the end bud and first two leaves of each new shoot and the term refers to the largest leaves. FOP contains fine, tender, young leaves that have been rolled with a good balance of correct 'tip' (the delicate end pieces of the leaf buds), which guarantees quality. The word 'pekoe' derives from the Chinese word pek-ho or baihao, and refers to the covering of tiny silvery hairs on the underside of the leaves of certain types of the tea bush. Orange comes, we think, from Holland's 'House of Orange', the royal family of the first European country to import and re-export tea and thus a name connected with the very best quality.

Orange pekoe (OP)

Contains long pointed leaves that are larger than FOP and have been harvested when the end buds are opening into leaves. Seldom contains 'tips'.

Golden flowery orange pekoe (GFOP)

This is FOP with 'golden tips' – the very end of the golden yellow leaf buds.

Tippy golden flowery orange pekoe (TGFOP)

This is FOP with a large proportion of golden tips.

Finest tippy golden flowery orange pekoe (FTGFOP)

This is exceptionally high-quality FOP.

Special finest tippy golden flowery orange pekoe (SFTGFOP)

This is the very best FOP.

Pekoe

This consists of shorter, coarser leaves than OP.

Flowery pekoe (FP)

Flowery Pekoe consists of leaves that have been rolled lengthwise and the pieces are shorter and coarser than OP.

Pekoe Souchong (PS)

This consists of shorter, coarser leaves than Pekoe.

Souchong (S)

The word 'souchong' means 'sub-variety' in Chinese, a term associated with large leaves that have been rolled lengthwise to produce ragged, coarse pieces. Souchong is often used for smoked teas from China and Taiwan.

Broken Leaf Grades are divided into the following categories:

- Golden Flowery Broken Orange Pekoe (GFBOP)
- Golden Broken Orange Pekoe (GBOP)
- Tippy Golden Broken Orange Pekoe (TGBOP)
- Tippy Flowery Broken Orange Pekoe (TFBOP)
- Tippy Golden Flowery Broken Orange Pekoe (TGFBOP)
- Flowery Broken Orange Pekoe (FBOP)
- Broken Orange Pekoe (BOP)
- Broken Pekoe Souchong (BPS)

Fannings

Fannings (also referred to as Fines or Dusts) are made up of the finest siftings left after the larger whole leaf and broken leaf particles have been removed. They are useful in blends for teabags, which require a quick brewing tea. The number 1 is also added to the broken leaf grades to denote the best quality (eg PF 1, Dust 1). Dusts and Fannings are further categorized as:

- Orange Fannings (OF)
- Broken Orange Pekoe Fannings (BOPF)
- Pekoe Fannings (PF)
- Broken Pekoe Fannings (BPF)
- Pekoe Dust (PD)

CTC teas are generally categorized as follows:

- Broken Pekoe (BP)
- Broken Pekoe 1 (BP1)
- Pekoe Fannings (PF)
- Fannings (F) or (FNGS)
- Pekoe Dust (PD)
- Dust (D)
- Dust 1 (D1)
- Dust 2 (D2)
- Red Dust (RD)
- Broken Mixed Fannings (BMF)

It is important to understand that grading terms only give information about the appearance and size of the leaf. It is impossible to tell if a tea is good or not without actually tasting it. The quality of each tea depends on the cultivation, processing, handling and storing of the leaf and it is essential to taste the tea to judge how good or bad it is.

Tea blends

Just like wine connoisseurs, tea connoisseurs enjoy the fact that the flavour and quality of different teas vary from year to year and from season to season because of inevitable changes in the weather or slight differences in the manufacturing process. They take pleasure in comparing a First Flush Darjeeling from, for example, Margaret's Hope Estate to a First Flush Darjeeling from Castleton, or a Second Flush Assam from Harmutty in 2008 to a Second Flush from Harmutty in 2007.

Yet some tea-drinkers prefer to know that each time they buy a particular tea, for example, English Breakfast or Earl Grey, Ceylon Blend or Darjeeling, it will always taste the same and give the same strength and flavour. It is for this reason that tea blenders and packers create blends to suit their customers. To do this they must taste hundreds of samples of different teas every day in order to find the mix of up to 35 different teas that will give that standard flavour. The blenders taste teas from different estates, different regions and different seasons and then create a recipe using the selected teas. It's a little like wine-blending or perfumery in that the ingredients vary in number and range but the final result must always be the same.

In order to assess the different teas, tea tasters prepare the samples by a strict set of rules. The dry leaf teas are set out in their containers in a long row on the tasting bench. A specific weight of each tea (usually 5.2–5.6g; 0.18–0.2oz) is then carefully measured into a special lidded brewing mug and boiling water for black teas, or slightly cooler water for green teas, is poured on. A timer is set and when the leaves have steeped for five to six minutes (sometimes shorter for certain green teas) the lidded mugs are tipped on their side in a tasting bowl and the serration in the lip of the mug allows the tea to run into the bowl. The wet leaves are knocked out onto the upturned lid of the mug and set close to the tasting bowl. The taster then uses a rounded spoon to slurp some of the tea sharply into the mouth so that it hits the taste buds. The liquor is rolled around the mouth to assess the full flavour before being spat out into a mobile spittoon that trundles along beside the work bench. When assessing the tea's quality and value, the taster takes into consideration the appearance of the dry leaf, the appearance and smell of the wet leaf, and the appearance, taste and aroma of the liquor.

Once the right recipe for a particular blend has been decided, the necessary teas are loaded into large, funnel-shaped containers (hoppers) which feed a blending drum where the teas are mixed thoroughly together. The blend is then packed in the usual way.

Classic Blends

Certain blends have developed over the centuries according to the preference of individual tea-drinking nationalities. The British have always liked a robust strong tea to wake them up in the morning and so English Breakfast blends have traditionally been made up of teas that give a rich flavour and a good, dark coppery colour. To create such a mixture, blenders choose from teas they know to have the appropriate characteristics.

English Breakfast

In Britain, this is almost always made up of a blend of teas from Assam, for its warm malty smoothness, Sri Lanka, for its brisk golden quality, and Kenya, for its strength and depth of flavour and colour. Some American companies use China Keemun teas exclusively as the base for their English Breakfast blends and the choice of teas depends very much on the personal preferences of individual blenders.

Irish Breakfast

The Irish like their tea very strong and dark and the blend is similar to English Breakfast but usually includes a greater proportion of Kenya tea and sometimes black teas from Indonesia.

Indian Breakfast

Usually a blend of Darjeeling and Assam, or Assam and Nilgiri, or a mixture of teas from all three areas. These blends tend to be lighter than English Breakfast blends and include the distinctive character of fruity, slightly astringent Darjeelings.

Earl Grey

Probably the most popular and well-known flavoured blend in the world, this is traditionally a blend of China black tea and essential oil of bergamot. Some tea companies today offer green, oolong and decaffeinated Earl Grey as well as black. Several stories, all of which relate to Earl Grey who was British prime minister from 1830 to 1834, have developed over the years to explain the origin of this famous tea, but it is impossible to know if any of them are true. One tale tells how a British diplomat, while on a mission to China during Earl Grey's premiership, saved the life of a mandarin and was given the recipe to take home to the prime minister as a symbol of gratitude. Another tells that it was the Earl himself who saved the Chinese nobleman. Yet another features the tea as a gift presented to Earl Grey at the end of a successful diplomatic visit to China. However, as far as we know, although the Chinese have flavoured their tea with many different extra ingredients over the centuries, bergamot is never mentioned as one of them and such colourful legends may simply have been an intelligent marketing ploy.

Russian Caravan

A blend of black teas from China that often has a slightly smoky flavour. This blend attempts to recreate the taste of the teas that were transported back to Moscow from the Chinese border after furs had been traded for tea. When the Chinese tea producers started making black teas in the seventeenth century for export to far-off lands such as Russia, America and England, the manufacturing process included drying the teas in large ovens fired with local pine wood. The smoke from the wood gave the teas a slightly smoky character and perhaps the teas acquired an even more smoky character from the camp fires that kept the caravan traders warm at night during their long journey back to St Petersburg. Whatever the reason for the smoky flavour, consumers in Russia grew to enjoy it and today, in order to replicate the smokiness, Russian Caravan blends usually include a small amount of smoky Lapsang Souchong in the mixture of black teas.

Afternoon Blend

Usually a blend of black teas from Sri Lanka and India but sometimes with added flavourings such as jasmine or bergamot. Some tea-blending companies prefer to create a very light tea for the afternoon and base the blend on Darjeeling or Chinese and Taiwanese teas.

Range of products from Tregothnan Tea Estate – Classic Tea, Afternoon Tea, Earl Grey, and Green Tea

Own blends

Blends can easily be created to suit different tastes, different times of the day and different foods. Successful blending is usually the result of experimentation and tasting, trial and error. Some people like to add a hint of Earl Grey to a favourite Ceylon or Assam, others like the smokiness of Lapsang Souchong added to their English Breakfast blend.

Teas can also be flavoured at home by the addition of a few dried flower petals, pieces of spice or dried herbs. Push a cinnamon stick into a caddy of black tea for a deliciously subtle cinnamon-flavoured tea, or add a whole vanilla pod to a tin of green Japanese Sencha for a slightly sweet, gently aromatic tea. Add dried mint leaves to green or black tea for a refreshing and soothing flavoured tea.

When creating own blends in large quantities, it is important to select teas with similar leaf sizes or the mixture will separate out in the packet or tin and give an uneven brew. So choose a Ceylon Orange Pekoe and a Kenyan Orange Pekoe to mix together; select a Broken Orange Pekoe Assam to blend with a Broken Orange Pekoe Ceylon; or mix an orthodox FOP or OP Darjeeling with an orthodox FOP or OP Nilgiri. If playing with flavours each time you brew, the size of leaf is not so crucial and you can simply try adding a pinch of Earl Grey to a favourite Ceylon, or a few leaves of Lapsang Souchong to Assam to give a touch of smokiness. Once blended, store the blend in an air-tight container in a dark, cool place, away from other smells. Flavoured teas can easily taint teas stored nearby so do make sure that packets and tins are really tightly sealed.

How tea is traded

The trading of tea has changed radically over the past fifty years. At one time, London was the centre of the tea trade, with vast quantities arriving by ship from China and tea being offered at the London auctions to international buyers. England's earliest recorded auction of tea took place in London on 11 March 1679 and by the mid-18th century quarterly auctions of China teas were being held. In 1706, the auctions took place at Lord Craven's House in Leadenhall Street in the City of London, which became known as East India House. The tea was sold 'by the candle', whereby a candle, marked out into inches, was lit as bidding began and when one inch had burned away the hammer was brought down on a particular lot. In 1834, the auctions moved premises to the newly built Commercial Salesrooms in nearby Mincing Lane and then in 1937 moved again to Plantation House, just down the road. In 1971, the auctions relocated to Sir John Lyon House in Upper Thames Street and again in 1990 to the London Chamber of Commerce.

Brewed teas in a tasting room. As well as tasting the tea liquor, tea tasters examine the dry leaf, the wet leaf and the appearance of the tea itself.

Because of the changing nature of the tea trade and the setting up of auction centres in the producing countries, the London auctions closed in 1998.

Meanwhile, the producing countries had set up their own auctions where locally grown teas were offered to local and international buyers. In 1861, India held its first tea auctions in Calcutta. India now has auction centres in Calcutta, Guwahati (1970), Siliguri, Cochin (1948), Coonoor (1963) and Coimbatore (1980); Sri Lanka's centre was established in Colombo in 1883; the Chittagong auctions opened in 1949 to sell Bangladeshi tea; Kenya's Nairobi auctions began in 1956 and moved to Mombasa in 1969 (the Mombasa auctions sell teas from Uganda, Rwanda, Burundi and Tanzania); Limbe in Malawi opened in 1970; and Jakarta's Indonesian tea auctions first traded in 1972. Some teas from those countries, as well as teas from countries where there are no auctions, are traded by private treaties drawn up between producers and brokers.

At J Thomas, tea brokers of Kolkata, tasters and colleagues sample teas ready for the weekly auctions.

Before an auction is held, samples of tea are sent out by the producing estates and gardens to potential customers who taste them and assess which, if any, they wish to buy. Bids are then made at the auction in the normal way (the tea itself is not actually at the auction but all those taking part have already tasted the samples and a catalogue lists all the lots on offer) and the purchased teas are transported from the producer's factory in the country of origin to the purchaser's warehouse.

The year 1982 saw the start of offshore auctions, whereby container-loads of tea are sold while still at sea. Samples are sent out in the usual way before potential buyers decide if they want to purchase the container-load. With easier and faster communications around the world today, the buying and selling of tea happens much more quickly than before the introduction of the internet. Purchasers can order teas direct from the producers, producers are paid much more quickly and the turnaround of tea is much quicker. Since the closure of the London auctions, there have also been experiments in selling tea by electronic auction via the internet but this has been slow to take off and, without the support of the major world buyers, new websites have struggled to survive. In 2004, the Tea Board of India became the latest to try this method of trading

tea but this way of buying tea has still not really caught on.

When tea was first traded to Europe and America, the loose leaf was packed into tea chests and the more fragile, large-leafed teas are still packed in this way but most bulk teas are today packed into multi-layer tough paper sacks. These are then loaded onto pallets, shrinkwrapped, placed inside containers, loaded onto container ships and dispatched to consuming countries all around the world. On arrival, the tea is unloaded and sent by truck to suitable warehousing facilities.

Most large tea blenders and packers buy vast quantities of tea from brokers and through auctions

At the factory, teas are bulked and packed in sturdy paper sacks, then palletized ready for transportation to the customer.

across the globe. They then blend the tea (see page 67) and pack it as teabags or loose packet tea, or they use it as a base for flavoured teas. Some tea companies have a close relationship with, or financial interests in, particular plantations and so buy direct from those estates. Small-scale traders usually buy smaller quantities of tea from brokers and wholesalers and then pack them into smaller quantities ready for sale to the consumer.

Instead of only selling their tea in bulk through auction centres, some plantations now sell what is known as 'value added tea' direct from the estates to their customers – who may include supermarket chains or agents working in the different consuming countries. 'Value added teas' are teas that have been packed into teabags or packets and caddies at the factory rather than in bulk. The selection of teas offered generally includes a blended tea typical of the region and a range of flavoured teas. The thinking behind this new approach is that it is worth investing in the necessary bagging and packaging machinery in order to raise the consuming public's awareness of particular teas from individual origins and to take control of the way in which the local tea reaches the consumer. When a producing country or region sells its bulk teas to a consuming country, those teas are almost always blended with teas from several other origins. The result is that consumers no longer have any idea how satisfyingly different the teas from different parts of the world taste and their freedom of choice is taken away. Single origin teas offer tea drinkers around the world an opportunity to savour the individual character of different teas.

Value-added teas also allow the individual producers to increase their profits. Furthermore, as happens today in Kenya, where the KTDA now produces small quantities of orthodox as well as CTC black teas, some producers of high-quality teas are now selling smaller quantities of their teas (two or three chests at a time) direct to small companies instead of putting all their tea into the auctions.

Tea packaging

Over the centuries, the packaging of tea has undergone major changes. Until the days of the Ming Dynasty (AD 1368–1644), China's compressed teas travelled well, wrapped in bamboo, dried grasses or banana leaves and the tablets, tea balls and slabs retained their shape, quality and flavour. But the fashion for loose-leaf tea that emerged during the Ming period meant that new packaging methods were required. Open bamboo baskets were useless and heavy earthenware jars and lacquered boxes were too cumbersome to be practical. And so the tea chest was invented. Cheaper types of tea were packed into bamboo crates lined with wax paper, rice paper and bamboo paper, while more expensive, delicate teas were packed into decorative lacquer chests. Now the Chinese merchants could send their teas on the 18-month journey across the high seas to Europe without worrying constantly for the safety and quality of the product. Chests were gradually improved to create a truly air-tight container but the change from various papers to a lead lining was later recognized as a health hazard and aluminium or tin foil was used instead.

Today, tea chests are only used for expensive large-leafed teas which are easily crushed and need considerable protection during shipping. Chests are often made from the timber of shade trees which grow amongst the tea plants on the plantations. These shade trees protect the bushes from the glare of intensive sunlight and need felling and replacing from time to time. This recycling of the wood helps to make the tea an environmentally ethical commodity. Some producers now use foil-lined boxes or cartons instead of wooden chests for their more fragile large-leaf teas and these vary in size and shape. For smaller-leafed varieties, chests and cartons have generally been replaced by paper sacks that are made from several layers of tough paper and aluminium foil, strong and thick enough to keep flavour in and humidity and odours out. There is no standard size for paper sacks and those in common usage can carry between 20 and 50kg (44–110lbs) of tea. For transportation, filled sacks are loaded onto pallets and wrapped tightly with several layers of shrinkwrap plastic.

In the retailing of tea, packaging has also changed dramatically over the centuries. In Europe, early consumers bought small quantities of tea in a 'screw' of paper. Merchants would sell 'straights' or blended teas – often specially made to individual clients' requirements. In the nineteenth century, with the market expanding and competition between merchants increasing rapidly, the idea of packaging loose tea in branded packets and boxes took off. For the first time, individual companies offered guaranteed exact weights and attracted customers by drawing on oriental images for the design of their caddies and packets. Today, teas are available in a wide variety of caddies, tins and boxes, cardboard packages, decorative wooden caskets, foil-lined pouches, vacuum-packed tubs and porcelain jars, the most important feature being tight lids that shut out the air.

Storing tea

The enemies of tea are humidity, air and light and it is extremely important that tea is carefully stored from the moment it leaves the drying machines in the factory to its arrival in the caddy or tin at home. Manufacturers must ensure that made tea is immediately transferred from drying and blending machines to sealed paper sacks or chests. The wholesaler must ensure that sacks and chests are kept closed and in cool, dry storage in the warehouse. Similarly, the retailer needs a clean, dry, cool storage space for spare stock and air-tight storage tins or caddies on shop shelves from which to sell to customers. Ready-packed tins and packages of tea must be tightly sealed (and preferably re-sealable) so that once the customer has taken the tea home, it is easy to keep the tea fresh and air-tight.

At home it is always best to transfer both loose tea and teabags from a cardboard or paper packet or tub into an air-tight container of some sort. Tins and caddies with really tight-fitting lids are best as they will keep out other smells and humidity. Air-tight glass jars on open shelves are not ideal for the storage of tea as light can damage the leaves and reduce the quality. If, however, the jars are stored in a dark cupboard, the tea will keep well. Tea should not be kept in the refrigerator as there is always a chance that water or water vapour will get into the packet. The only exception to this rule is Japanese Matcha, the powdered green tea used in the Japanese Tea Ceremony (see page 86). This tea does not keep well and small amounts are sold in vacuum-sealed containers that, in Japan, are usually kept in the refrigerator.

Be extra careful with flavoured teas. The added flavourings can be very powerful and easily taint other teas nearby. Similarly, take care when measuring tea from caddy or packet to teapot. Make sure that the spoon or scoop used is absolutely dry. If there is even a drop of moisture on the spoon, the humidity introduced to the interior of the packet or caddy will have a damaging effect on the quality and flavour.

Teas must be stored in air-tight tins in cool, dry conditions.

Choosing what to buy

With the increasingly wide variety of teas available today, it is sometimes difficult to decide what to buy. Ultimately, only by trying different types of tea will an individual tea-drinker be able to decide what he or she likes best for particular occasions. Wherever possible, buy small quantities of a tea to sample before buying larger quantities. Go to a retail store that can offer guidance and advice. Ask lots of questions about the tea itself, the best way to brew, how to store, whether the tea drinks well with milk, etc, and be aware of grading terms used on retailers' packets and tins. If you are not sure what they mean, ask more questions. A good retailer will be happy to discuss the different teas with you. Be aware also that the nature of the water in a particular region or country will make a difference to your experience of any one tea.

A display of teas, herbs and tea-brewing equipment at a small tea store in Tibet.

Brewing Tea

The first important decision to be made when choosing a tea is whether to buy teabags or loose-leaf. Many people prefer teabags because they are easier to handle, the quantity of tea is already measured out, they do not present the problem of how to dispose of the wet leaves, they allow for the easy removal of the bag from the brew once the correct strength has been achieved and are generally convenient and quick to use. Some teabags are extremely disappointing because of the small amount and poor quality of the leaf inside the bag. However, there are companies that do offer very good teabags containing quality leaf. The latest trend is for bags made of nylon gauze (often referred to as 'crystal') or muslin. As well as being extremely sophisticated and stylish, these bags usually contain larger grades of leaf and allow the tea enough room to swell up and release its flavour and colour more successfully into the water.

Many true tea connoisseurs intensely dislike the idea of teabags and prefer always to choose a loose leaf. The advantages, as they see it, are that a much wider selection of loose-leaf teas is available from around the world, the brewer can decide what quantity and quality of tea to use, loose tea almost always gives a better, more subtle and fuller-flavoured brew than teabags and, for the connoisseur, the ritual of measuring out the leaves into the pot is an important part of the tea-brewing ceremony.

The case for teabags or loose tea

Advantages of teabags
- easy to brew just one cup;
- quick and convenient;
- easy to separate tea from liquor once the brew has reached the correct strength;
- no untidy wet leaves to dispose of;
- useful for brewing large quantities of tea for special events, etc.

Disadvantages of most types of teabags

- do not offer the wide selection of world teas that are available as loose tea;
- contain small particles of tea that brew quickly but often lack subtlety of flavour (nylon gauze bags do now allow larger grades of leaf to be bagged);
- often do not allow the tea enough room to brew properly;
- the paper of the teabag stops the full flavour of the tea infusing out into the water;
- teabags lose their flavour and quality more quickly than loose-leaf tea;
- only small-leafed teas can be put into most types of teabag.

Advantages of loose-leaf tea

- the consumer has an endless choice of world teas;
- the decision of how much tea to use is left to the consumer;
- the measuring of the leaf is a very important part of the traditional tea-brewing ceremony;
- the consumer can assess the quality of a tea from the appearance and aroma of the wet leaves as well as from the taste of the liquor.

Disadvantages of loose-leaf tea

- if leaf tea is allowed to brew for too long the liquor will become bitter and harsh; it is preferable to separate the leaves from the water at the end of the correct brewing time by lifting out the infuser basket or by straining the tea liquor from the brewing pot into a second, clean, warm pot;
- perfect brewing needs the correct temperature of water, careful measuring of the leaf and timing of the brew – this is not actually a disadvantage at all, but simply a vital element in the performance of brewing.

Water for tea

The type of water used for brewing plays an enormously important role in the final flavour, clarity and colour of the liquor. While a tea brewed in one particular water may taste dull and flat, the same tea brewed in water from a different location can be wonderfully brisk and bright. All the ingredients of an individual water play their part in the brewing process – the natural minerals, the added chemicals such as chlorine and fluoride, the amount of oxygen, etc.

To remove unwanted solubles, mains water needs to be passed through some kind of filtration system. Some filtration systems add various salts and minerals to the water and these can create different problems. The most effective types work according to a process known as 'reverse osmosis', whereby the water is passed through a membrane which forces unwanted chemicals and other deposits out of the water molecules to leave water that is approximately 99.4 per cent pure.

LuYu (see page 7) recommended spring water as the best for tea because of its purity, freshness and high oxygen content. The poorest water for tea is water that has stood for any length of time and has therefore become lifeless and flat.

Hard water which contains a high level of calcium is poor for most types of tea, deadening the flavour and causing a scum to form on the surface of the tea in the cup, as calcium carbonate reacts with oxygen to become calcium bicarbonate. The addition of acid to the tea helps to eliminate the bicarbonate ions, and so adding a drop or two of lemon juice prevents scum from being formed. Adding sugar to the tea also reduces the development of scum but most teas are better without sugar and so this is not recommended.

If soft water and permanently hard water (that contains calcium sulphate) are used for tea, the liquor is usually bright and clear and the flavour brisk and lively. If bottled water is used, a pH of 7 is ideal. But choose carefully since many types of bottled water contain salts and other minerals which can spoil the flavour of the tea in the same way as can some tap water.

Teas through the day

The wide variety of teas available today means that each individual tea-drinker can choose something to suit the palate, time of day, food being served, mood, season, weather. Everyone has a favourite early-morning tea, a tea to drink by the fire on a dark and dismal winter afternoon, an evening tea to enjoy after a wonderful dinner. There are no firm rules as to which tea should be drunk when, but here are some guidelines:

First thing in the morning and at breakfast choose a strong black tea that gives a gentle dose of caffeine and helps get the brain and body going, such as English Breakfast, Irish Breakfast, Assam, Kenya or Yunnan. These have a strength and depth that marry well with the strong flavours of cooked breakfast foods and with breads and pastries served with preserves or honey.

Mid-morning and at lunchtime choose a tea that will continue to help you concentrate and perform well through the working day. Any of the morning teas work well, or choose smoky Lapsang Souchong, flavoury Ceylon, China Keemun or Nilgiri. If lunch consists of oriental food, choose a green Sencha or Chinese Chun Mee or Gunpowder.

As the afternoon progresses turn to lighter teas that offer a fragrance and gentleness to soothe and calm – perhaps a peachy oolong, a fruity Darjeeling, a lighter Ceylon, any variety of green tea, or a flavoured tea such as mango or peach.

At afternoon tea choose teas that pair well with the food offered. Earl Grey goes extremely well with cheese sandwiches or savouries, and with lemon cake or lemon tarts; Darjeeling is excellent with anything creamy so is perfect with scones and clotted cream; Lapsang Souchong is wonderful with smoked salmon or smoked chicken sandwiches; a brisk Ceylon enhances fresh fruit or sandwiches made with cucumber, tomatoes and other salad ingredients; strong Kenya and English Breakfast blends are great with chocolate cakes, rich truffles and chocolate cheesecakes.

In the evening perfect teas are the lighter oolongs, greens and whites. These are very cleansing after a meal and offer an elegance and cleanness that is good after dinner and before sleep. These are also teas that drink well alone, without food, and create just the right mood for the time of day when life begins to slow down.

Equipment for preparing tea

Tea wares designed by Paul Smith for The Berkeley Hotel, London.

The teapot

The teapots used in the West today developed from the little round-bodied teapots that were imported from China to Europe and North America on the same ships that brought the tea. Whereas coffee pots have always been tall and usually straight-sided, teapots have retained their low, squat shape. The early imported pots were small because that is how the Chinese made and used their pots (and indeed still use them today), but as the cost of tea in Europe fell during the eighteenth and nineteenth centuries and tea became more of an everyday beverage, teapots grew in size.

The best teapots are those made in glazed stoneware, pottery, china, porcelain and glass. Silver tewares have been popular since the late seventeenth century but silver does not necessarily make the best brewing vessel. Silver can hold the flavour of the last tea brewed in it and so needs very careful washing and rinsing after use.

Teapots that are glazed inside can be washed in a dishwasher or by hand using normal detergents. However, to be sure that the flavour of brewed tea is not tainted with residues of soap, always rinse the teapot very carefully. To restore a tea's flavour and aroma to a pot, spoon in a scoop of dry tea leaves, place the lid on the pot and leave to stand until the next time it is used, then empty out the dry leaves before the pot is re-used.

To remove tea stains from the inside and spout of a teapot, measure in two large spoonfuls of bicarbonate of soda, fill the pot with boiling water and leave to soak overnight. Rinse thoroughly and dry. Commercial cleaning products, such as Buster TSR (Tea and Coffee Stain Remover) are very effective but be sure to rinse the pot well before re-using.

Yixing teapots

Yixing is famous for its many coloured clays and for the teapots made from them. Since the 1500s, potters in this Chinese lakeside town have been fashioning the most exquisite unglazed teapots in the form of houses, lotus flowers, pumpkins, Buddhist priests, boxes, bundles of bamboo, dragons, fruit, vegetables, human figures and buildings. Yixing pots are said to be the best brewing vessels for oolong

teas and because the interior of the pot is unglazed, each pot must only be used for one tea. Over time, the pot absorbs the flavour of the tea and builds up a patina that enhances future brews. For this reason, a Yixing pot should never be washed with soaps and detergents but should simply be rinsed and allowed to dry.

Infuser and plunger teapots

The flavour of tea can become very unpleasant if the leaves stand for too long in the hot water, so many different pots are now available that contain their own purpose-designed infuser basket that can be lifted out, or that have a plunger (rather like the plunger in a cafetière) that allows the separation of the tea from the liquor once the tea has brewed.

When choosing a pot with an inbuilt infuser, make sure that the infuser basket or bag is large enough to allow the leaves to move around, swell up and release their colour and flavour into the water, and check that the design allows the lid to sit neatly on the top of the pot both when the infuser is in the pot and after it has been lifted out. If choosing a plunger pot, make sure that the plunger really does separate the leaves from the water. As long as any of the leaves are in contact with the water, the tea will go on brewing.

Infusers

Also available today is a range of plastic, metal, cloth and paper infusers that allow the easy separation of the leaf from the water.

Aluminium is not good as a material for these infusers as it taints the flavour of the tea, but chrome, porcelain, nylon, plastic, unbleached paper are all excellent — as long as they are large enough to allow the tea to brew properly. They should be designed so that they fit down into the bottom of the teapot, are easy to handle and easy to lift out once the tea has brewed.

Infuser mugs are also available. These act like a mini teapot and are a useful alternative in the workplace or kitchen.

The guywan

The *Guywan* (mandarin Chinese for 'covered cup'; in Cantonese, *Cha Chung* or *Zhong*) is one of China's traditional brewing vessels. It consists of a deep bowl that has no handle, a lid and a saucer. The loose tea leaves are measured into the guywan, water is added and, with the lid in place, the leaves are allowed to brew. The liquor is then drunk from the cup while the lid is carefully angled to hold the leaves back inside the cup.

Japanese tea bowls

The large, rather rough, handmade pottery bowls used for whisked tea during the Japanese Tea Ceremony have been made in the same way since the Japanese started drinking tea almost 1,200 years ago. They are thought to have developed from Korean rice bowls and, since most potters in Japan at that time came from Korea, it was this style that was adapted for tea. The bowls must be of a certain thickness; if they are too thin they will be too hot to hold and may allow the tea to cool too rapidly. Conversely, bowls that are too thick will not become sufficiently hot.

Tea hotplates

Several companies now offer glass or metal hotplates on which to keep brewed tea warm. These should never be too hot and the little candle lights designed for use in them are ideal. However, tea kept warm in this way will deteriorate after about 25 minutes and be sure never to stand a pot of tea on one of these special burners if the leaves are still in the pot.

Tea cosies

Tea cosies are useful for keeping a pot of tea warm but should never be used if the tea leaves are still in the pot, as the tea may become bitter and unpleasant.

Caddy spoons and scoops

The ideal scoop or measure for spooning tea from caddy or packet to pot holds approximately 2.5g (0.09oz). The perfect measure for most teas is 2. 5–3g (0.09–0.10oz) of tea to 190–200ml (6½–7fl oz) of water. This varies according to the type of tea used and to personal taste.

Brewing methods

The method of brewing tea differs according to the individual tea and to the traditional tea culture of the country in question.

Brewing black tea in a teapot

1. Select a teapot of the correct size for the number of cups required.
2. Fill a kettle or pan with freshly drawn cold water and bring to the boil.
3. When the water is almost boiling, pour a little into the teapot, swill it around and then pour the water away.
4. Measure the loose tea or count the teabags (allowing one bag per cup to be brewed) into the teapot and when the water in the kettle is just coming to a rolling boil, pour the water onto the leaves or bags. Whenever possible, place the leaves inside an infuser that can then be lifted out of the liquid once the tea has brewed. Allow 2.5–3g (0.09–0.10oz) of tea per 190–200ml (6½–7fl oz) water.
5. Put the lid on the pot and set a timer to the correct number of minutes for the tea being brewed. For small-leafed teas, allow 2–3 minutes, for large-leafed teas, allow 3–5 minutes, depending on personal taste.
6. After the correct number of minutes, lift the infuser containing the leaves out of the pot and discard. If not using an infuser, immediately strain all the tea into cups or into another heated pot to keep warm. Discard the leaves, or

if the tea is of a variety that will give a second and possibly a third infusion, add more water and leave to brew for the required number of minutes.
7. Keep the pot warm on a special hotplate that is heated by a candle light or cover the pot with a cosy. Never keep a pot of tea hot in this way if the leaves are still in the pot – the tea will stew and taste extremely bitter and unpleasant.

Brewing puerh teas

Most puerh teas yield up to nine or ten infusions and so, although the leaf can be very expensive, it does offer very good value for money.

1. Bring freshly drawn cold water to the boil and warm the vessel in which the tea is to be brewed.
2. Measure 3–5g (0.10–0.18oz) of tea into the pot or the guywan and add 200ml (7fl oz) of boiling water. Infuse for only 10–20 seconds then strain the liquor off the leaf. Add more water up to ten times and allow to steep for 10–20 seconds each time, reducing the steeping time slightly for each infusion.

Brewing green tea in a teapot

Follow the steps for brewing black tea but never pour boiling water onto green tea. Green leaves prefer a cooler temperature so use a temperature-controlled kettle or pour water from a boiling kettle, urn or still into an empty pot or jug and allow to cool before pouring onto the

the tea. Use a thermometer to check the temperature of the water before pouring onto the tea. Ideal temperatures for green teas vary from 50–85°C (122–185°F), depending on the individual tea.

Brewing times for green teas vary. Most Chinese greens need 3–4 minutes in water at 70–85°C (158–185°F), while Japanese teas brew very quickly and need to be separated from the water after 1–2 minutes or less. Some of Japan's most expensive green teas need water at 50–60°C (122–140°F).

Brewing white tea

The brewing time for different white teas varies. Some need 4–6 minutes while others may need up to 10 minutes. Chinese white teas generally need 5–6 minutes for the first steeping and slightly longer for subsequent steepings. Darjeeling whites need only 3–5 minutes.

Some white teas will yield more infusions than others. A good-quality Yin Zhen (Silver Needles) will give up to five or six infusions and each will have its own unique individual character. A Darjeeling white will give two or three infusions.

1. Bring freshly drawn cold water to the boil and allow it to cool to the same temperature as for oolong teas (so as not to scald the leaf). This is about 85–88°C (185–190°F).

2. Measure the leaves into a teapot, glass or guywan, allowing 2–3g (0.07–0.10oz) of leaf to 190–200ml (6½–7fl oz) of water.

3. Pour on the water, cover and allow to brew for between 3 and 10 minutes, depending on the type of tea.

4. Strain and add more water for further infusions.

The Chinese guywan

This is suitable for brewing white, green and oolong teas.

1. Start by rinsing the leaves. To do this, measure the tea into the guywan and pour on hot water at the correct temperature for the type of tea. Using the lid to hold the leaves back, tip away all the water. Lift off the lid and inhale the wonderful aroma of the leaves.

Silver kettle made in China in the late nineteenth century for the British market

A theatrical performance of the Gongfu tea ceremony in China.

2. Add more water to the cup, allowing it to run down the inside of the vessel rather than pouring it directly onto the leaves. This makes the leaves swirl in the cup and helps them to brew correctly.
3. Cover the guywan with its lid and allow the leaves to brew for the correct number of minutes: 1 for oolong, 3–4 for green.
4. To drink the tea, lift the three pieces of the guywan together and place comfortably in the palm of the right hand, using the thumb to hold the cup steady. With the first and second fingers and thumb of the left hand, lift the lid and tilt it so that it restrains the leaves inside the cup as the cup is tipped for drinking. The position of

the thumb against the nose during sipping hinders the drinker from tilting the cup too far. This is good because the guywan should not be completely emptied but should have more water added while some of the infusion is still in the cup.
5. Go on adding fresh hot water as many times as the tea leaves allow.

The Chinese 'Gongfu' method of brewing

The 'gongfu' brewing method allows the preparation of several short infusions from one measure of leaves, each infusion having its own distinct character. It should be carried out using a small Yixing earthenware teapot. You also need tall, straight-sided smelling cups, small, shallow drinking bowls and a waterproof tray on which to place all the equipment (waterproof because the various vessels are heated while standing on the tray by having hot water poured over them). With a traditional set of brewing equipment, the tray has its own draining device to carry away the water.

1. Start by pouring hot water into the little teapot to warm it and then pour that water away.
2. For brewing black, oolong and puerh teas by this method rinse the leaves and prepare them for the brewing process. Measure the tea leaves into the pot (2.5–3g; 0.09–0.10oz) per 190–200ml (6½–7fl oz) and pour in enough hot or boiling water to half fill it. Place the lid on the pot and drain off all the liquid. For green tea, leave out this rinsing stage of the brewing ceremony.
3. Warm the little drinking bowls by pouring hot water into them and then draining the water out.
4. Add more water to the teapot, put the lid on the pot and pour more water over the pot. For oolong tea allow about 1 minute, for green tea allow 2–3 minutes and for black tea allow 3 minutes.
5. Immediately strain the tea liquor into a second teapot or bowl before pouring it into the tall, straight-sided smelling cups.
6. Place a small drinking bowl upside down on top of the smelling cup and invert it carefully so that the tea flows into the drinking bowl.

The aroma of the tea can then be enjoyed in the smelling cup and the tea may be sipped from the little bowl.

7. Add more water to the leaves in the pot for a second and third infusion.

Brewing Japanese green tea

For a good-quality Sencha, choose a small teapot and small drinking bowls.

1. Bring freshly drawn water to the boil and pour some into the pot and bowls to warm them. Leave for 30–40 seconds and then pour the water away.
2. Measure about 2 teaspoons of tea into the pot and pour on approximately 200ml (7fl oz) of hot water at 80°C (176°F).
3. Allow to steep for 1–2 minutes then pour into the warmed bowls, pouring a little into each and then topping up with more tea from the pot so that each cup gets an even distribution of flavour.
4. Add more hot water to the leaves and allow to steep for a further 3 minutes to give a second, slightly stronger infusion.

With lower-quality Sencha, use water at approximately 90°C (194°F) and allow the tea to steep for only 30–60 seconds. For Bancha, Houjicha and Genmaicha, use a larger pot, boiling water and a short infusing time of not more than 30 seconds. For Gyokuro, use water at 60°C (140°F) and steep for not more than 2 minutes. Add more water and steep the second infusion for ½–1 minute.

Preparing tea for the Japanese tea ceremony

The tea used for the traditional Japanese Tea Ceremony is a fine green-powdered tea called Matcha (see page 173). To prepare Matcha, you need a traditional tea bowl, a tea scoop (called a *chashaku*) and a bamboo whisk (called a *chasen*). If you don't have these, use a teaspoon and a metal whisk.

1. Bring some water to the boil and then allow to cool.
2. Pour some hot water into the bowl and place the whisk in the water to warm it. After a few minutes, pour away the water. Scoop one and a half chashaku measures or two-thirds of a teaspoon of Matcha into the bowl.
3. Pour on a quarter of a bowl of the cooled water – the perfect temperature is 70–80°C (158–176°F) – and whisk briskly until little bubbles form on the surface of the tea.

Milk in tea

In the early days of tea-drinking in Britain, milk was not a regular addition to the cup. The custom seems to have started at the end of the seventeenth century and perhaps developed because milk and cream were found to soften the slightly bitter taste of tea. The Dutch drank what they called 'melk-thee', perhaps as a result of their contact with the Manchu Dynasty that was ruling China at the time when contact between the two countries began. A Dutch traveller, Jean Nieuhoff, wrote of his experience of tea with milk at a banquet given by the Chinese emperor for a visiting Dutch delegation in 1655. 'At the beginning of dinner,' he wrote, 'there were served several bottles of The or tea... This drink is made of the Herb The or Cha in fair water which afterwards they boil until a third part be consumed, to which they adde warm milk about a forth part, with a little salt, and then . . . drink it as hot as they can well endure.' In France, Madame de Sévigné told a friend in a letter that she drank her tea with milk and recommended the beverage to her daughter, suggesting both milk and sugar.

In Britain, the custom of adding milk to all types of tea was common by the middle of the eighteenth century and subsequently spread to the British colonies. The habit of course raises an important question – should the milk be poured into the tea or the tea into the milk? The answer depends on class, region, style of brewing and, of course, personal taste! Some will say that etiquette demands that the milk should be added to the tea and argue that it is more genteel and allows control of colour and strength, etc. (It is true that in the upper circles of Victorian society, poured cups of tea were handed to guests by the hostess or servants and the guests asked to help themselves to milk or cream and sugar.) Those in favour of 'milk in first' claim that this makes for a better mixing of the two fluids. There is also a belief that if cold milk is poured into boiling tea, there is a slight risk of spoiling the flavour of the brew by caramelizing the fat in the milk. Scientific experiments have in fact shown that this can happen and also that tiny globules of fat from the milk can remain floating on the surface of the cup of tea. But there is no easy answer to this point of debate and each individual tea-drinker must decide which method is best.

Tea-leaf reading

For hundreds of years, the art of tea-leaf reading has fascinated and entranced tea-drinkers. Many people believe that the wet tea leaves scattered in the cup after the tea has been drunk are as good a guide to future events as the reading of palms and tarot cards.

Tasseology is an intuitive art married with psychic skills that enables the reader to see into the future. As leading tasseologist, Amber McCarroll, says in her book, *The Magic in Tea Leaves*, 'universal symbolism . . . acts as a pictorial shorthand for the subconscious and we can all benefit from developing this forgotten skill'. The information gained from a tea-leaf reading usually applies only to the 24 hours immediately following the reading and for the best results, the reader must only look for answers to specific questions. A reading is only relevant to whoever has drunk from the cup.

- To prepare the cup, make a pot of tea in the usual way. Larger leaves are best as they create a more revealing mixture of images and patterns.
- Pour a cup of tea without using a strainer, so that some of the leaves go into the cup with the liquor.
- Drink the tea in the usual way but leave about a teaspoonful of liquid in the bottom of the cup with the leaves.

The drinker then holds the cup in the left hand with the rim upwards and turns it fast three times in an anti-clockwise direction. The drinker tips the cup onto a saucer and allows the tea to drain into the saucer before turning the cup the right way up again and handing it to the reader.

The reader holds the cup with the handle pointing towards the body and tries to interpret the significance of the leaves, and so help the drinker relate the pattern to specific aspects of their life – and to the specific question being asked. Leaves scattered near the handle represent personal and home life. Leaves to the left of the handle represent the past and leaves to the right indicate the future. Those on the opposite side of the cup represent far-off events and people, while those in the bottom are to do with difficult emotions. The area around the rim signifies happy times and positive events and the ring that runs halfway around the inside of the cup is connected with everyday emotions and events. The reader focuses on a particular area of the cup according to the nature of the question being asked.

teas from around the world

The directory

The following pages are a guide to 122 world teas. For each one, the tea is shown as a dry leaf, a wet leaf, and an infusion (unless otherwise marked). The quantities of tea and the temperatures and brewing times recommended in the directory are only guidelines and teas will react differently in different types of water. Any of the recommendations can be adjusted to suit individual taste. For example, if a particular green tea is bitter or harsh, try reducing the water temperature and the brewing time.

Tea-growing areas on this and subsequent maps are denoted in green.

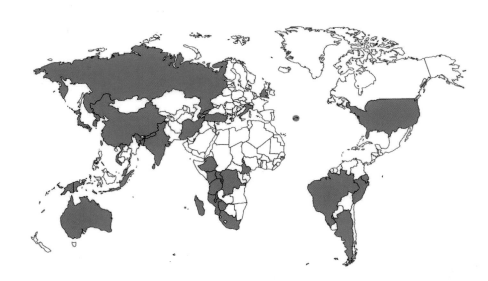

Bangladesh

Tea production in Bangladesh dates back to 1857 when the first garden was planted out at Malnicherra in Sylhet. Lying between the Khasia Hills and Jiantia Hills to the north and the Tripura Hills to the south, Sylhet is today home to 162 tea estates that stretch for miles and miles across the rolling countryside. From 40 million kg (44,093 tons) in 1980, production has now reached 60 million kg (66,139 tons) but, with increasing domestic demand accounting for the consumption of the majority of that, only about 12 million kg (13,228 tons) are left for export. Bangladesh teas are all black, give good colour, have a strong, sometimes slightly spicy character and are useful for strong, black blends such as English Breakfast. It is hoped that, with modernization of factories, improved infrastructure and a recently developed clonal variety of the tea plant, that the quantity of tea available for foreign exchange will gradually increase. The Bangladesh Tea Research Institute has developed a new, high-yielding clone that produces much more tea per hectare than other varietals and gives a strong, juicy liquor. Normal production per hectare is approximately 1,270 kg (1.4 ton) of tea but the new clone, BT16, yields more than 3,000 kg (3.3 tons) per hectare and if all the gardens in the country gradually replant with this clone, the tea industry will become even more important to the country's economy.

Other developments have been in the production of organic teas and, working closely with the Bangladesh Tea Board, the Kazi & Kazi Tea Estate Ltd started growing organic teas in 2000 in the northerly district of Panchagargh and now produces both orthodox and CTC organic teas for overseas and local markets.

Kazi & Kazi Organic Golden Tippy Black

Character
Kazi & Kazi Tea Estate is in Tetulia
in the northernmost district of
Panchagargh. It planted its first teas
in 2000 on land that had previously
lain fallow, with the aim of bringing
the land and the community back to
life. Cultivation methods are
organic, production is both CTC
and orthodox and the estate also
makes hand-crafted white and green
teas. This elegant, twisted orthodox
tippy leaf yields a dark, intense
golden liquor with a spicy aroma
and a mouth-filling, brisk strength
with lingering spicy notes.

Brewing Tips
Brew 2.5–3g (0.09–0.10oz) in 200ml
(7fl oz) of boiling water for 3 minutes.

Organic Golden Tippy Black cup

Organic Golden Tippy Black dry

Organic Golden Tippy Black wet

Kazi & Kazi Organic Large Leaf

Character
Also from Tetulia in Panchagargh, the impressive, large twisty leaves give a golden amber liquor that has an earthy aroma and a sweet maltiness that is found in Assam teas with hints of black cherry.

Brewing Tips
Brew 2.5–3g (0.09–0.10oz) in 200ml (7fl oz) of boiling water for 3 minutes.

Organic Large Leaf cup

Organic Large Leaf dry

Organic Large Leaf wet

Bolivia

Bolivia is not widely known for its teas but local farmers are today making black, green and jasmine teas that are being distributed in the US by Simpson & Vail in Connecticut. Bolivian tea cultivation began in Larecaja province of the Department of La Paz in the late 1930s when German and Dutch companies established plantations and hand-crafted processing in an area that offered ideal conditions in terms of altitude, climate, rainfall and soil conditions. In 1976, an agreement between the governments of Bolivia and Taiwan led to increased plantings and the construction of three factories in Caranavi, Chimate and Chapare, and support for these operations continued until 1985. By 1993, the factory in Chimate had closed down due to changes in administration and lack of funding but was privatized in 1996 and continued its operations until the end of 2001 when it closed again. Then, in May 2005, with pressure from the tea farmers and demands for economic and social development, funding was obtained from the United States Agency for International Development (USAID),

the company Empresa Boliviana de Tés Especiales – ChaiMate SA – was established to revive the industry. Bushes were rehabilitated, green tea production lines installed, farmer field schools established, organic certification obtained, tea nurseries constructed and areas under cultivation expanded. Today, more than 200 farming families are benefiting from the revival of tea production with many other people working in the industry also enjoying increased earnings and higher standards of living. ChaiMate's chief sponsor is Fundacion Tropico Humedo, a non-profit body that supports the agricultural and technological development of the tropical forests of Bolivia, and the aims of the company are to increase sustainable human, social and economic development in the area through the manufacture of high grown, organic, speciality black, green and green jasmine teas. The teas available are whole leaf and broken orthodox blacks, steamed greens and jasmine greens scented with blossoms gathered from bushes that were established in the 1970s with help from the Taiwanese.

Bolivian Organic Green Jasmine

Character
Attractive, olive-green leaves give a bright greeny-yellow liquor, powerful jasmine aroma and wonderful perfumed jasmine taste.

Brewing Tips
Brew 2.5–3g (0.09–0.10oz) in 200ml (7fl oz) of water at 80°C (176°F) for 2 minutes.

Organic Green Jasmine cup

Organic Green Jasmine dry

Organic Green Jasmine wet

Bolivian Organic Green

Character
Unusually long, olive green leaves give a pale blue-green liquor that has a soft herbal aroma and a clean, smooth, sweet taste rather like a good Japanese green.

Brewing Tips
Brew 2.5g (0.09oz) in 200ml (7fl oz) of water at 80°C (176°F) for 3 minutes.

Organic Green cup

Organic Green dry

Organic Green wet

Bolivian Organic Large Leaf Black

Character
Beautiful, wiry, long black
leaves yield a bright amber
liquor that has a fresh, floral
aroma and a full-bodied, fruity
taste with lingering hints of
apricot and peach.

Brewing Tips
Brew 2.5g (0.09oz) in 200ml
(7fl oz) of boiling water for
3–4 minutes

Organic Large Leaf Black cup

Organic Large Leaf Black dry

Organic Large Leaf Black wet

Brazil

Chinese tea seeds were first planted at the Botanical Gardens of Rio De Janeiro in 1881 and the first commercial experiments were carried out by Chinese experts on the hills surrounding Rio shortly after that date but did not prosper. In the 1920s, Japanese immigration to the area led to a new surge of interest and a farmer by the name of Torazo Okamoto, who had experience of green tea production prior to his arrival in Brazil, made his first Brazilian green tea in 1925 and his first black tea in 1928. He brought Japanese tea-making machinery and Assam tea seeds into Brazil and most of the bushes cultivated today are descendants of those original seeds.

Today, the tea estates are located in the area of Minas Gerias around Registro, approximately two and a half hours' drive to the south-west of Sao Paulo. The factories are owned by descendants of the Japanese families who settled here in the early twentieth century and, although some closed during the 1990s due to economic pressures, some are still operating successfully. Private company, Sociedade Brasiliera Beneficiadora de Cha Ltda owns two companies, Yamatea and Chabras, and works very closely with Amaya, a third private company. Most of the green leaf is supplied by smallholder farmers who use mechanical harvesters to gather the leaf from approximately 3.5 million bushes. The country produces 3.2 million kg (3527 tons) of black tea annually, almost all of which is used to make iced tea and as an ingredient of English Breakfast-type blends. Production has fallen in recent years as farmers have found tea uneconomic compared to other crops.

The season runs from spring in October to autumn in May and the teas are all CTC black and have a very attractive biscuity, desiccated coconut character. Roughly 10 per cent of the tea is consumed within Brazil, about 70 per cent is exported to the USA and the rest is bought by European companies for use in their blends.

Brazil Amaya

Character
Neat CTC black leaf gives a
liquor that is rich bronze in
colour, has a sweet, flirtatious
coconut aroma and the easy,
smooth taste of crumbly
coconut biscuits.

Brewing Tips
Brew 2.5g (0.09oz) in 200ml
(7fl oz) of boiling water for
2–3 minutes.

Amaya cup

Amaya dry

Amaya wet

China

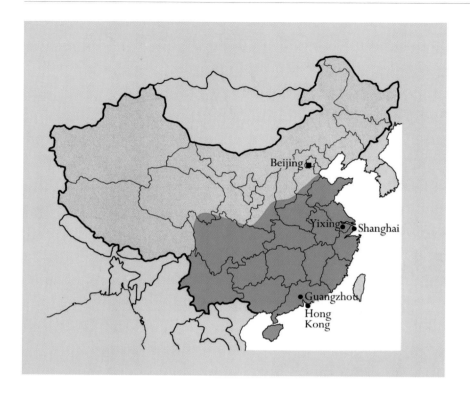

I n the early days of cultivation in China, small plantations were often tended by Buddhist monks on land around their mountain-top temples and monasteries, and since the Chinese have always believed that 'famous teas come from high mountains', these plantations often produced some of the finest and best known teas.

In the past, strict rules governed the manual gathering of the new leaf buds and leaves. The timing of the harvest was crucial and all teas were gathered before the spring rains

encouraged fast growth of the new shoots. The pickers were always young girls who would go out into the plantations in small groups very early in the morning and gather the young tender leaves into wicker baskets. It was vital that these pickers had immaculately clean fingernails and that they never ate garlic, onions, or other strongly flavoured foods that could change the smell of their skin and contaminate the teas they picked. Once the teas had been processed and packed, Chinese merchants sold more than 8,000 different types of

In China, the leaf is brought home by whatever means is available – on foot or by bicycle, motor bike or truck.

tea, which were classified by the different methods of manufacture, by region and by leaf grade.

Today, China produces about 18 per cent of world tea exports and a variety of teas are grown and produced in 16 different regions — Anhui, Fujian, Guangdong, Guangxi Zhuang, Guizhou, Hainan, Henan, Hubei, Hunan, Jiangsu, Jiangxi, Shaanxi, Shandong, Sichuan, Yunnan and Zhejiang. During the cold winter months, the tea bushes stop growing and start to flush again in the early spring. The season in China runs from March to late September and the best teas are made from leaf buds and leaves that are gathered in the spring from the high mountain areas.

The names by which the different teas are sold can be confusing. Names may give information about the garden where the tea grew, the time of year when the leaves were picked, the village or province, the method of manufacture used, any additional flavourings blended with the leaves and perhaps also a legendary name. Further confusions arise because the Chinese refer to what we call 'black' tea as 'red' and because there are different dialectical languages and spellings used in the different regions. Names may be in Fukienese, which is spoken in Fujian; Cantonese, which is spoken in Canton; or English, if a particular type of tea has been marketed by that name since trade with Europe began. For example, *Meigui Hongcha* in Pinyin is *Mui Kwai Hung Cha* in Cantonese but the tea is usually marketed as Rose Pouchong or Rose Black. And Pinyin *Tie Guanyin* becomes *Tit Koon Tam* in

Sorting through the leaves to remove any damaged leaves, twigs and weeds before manufacture.

Cantonese, *Ti KwanYin* for the international market, and translates as Tea of the Iron Goddess of Mercy. As well as its individual name, each tea is also given a grade number that indicates to customers that the tea is of a given standard. And some retailers and suppliers also add a 'chop' mark to their packaging that gives further information about the type of bush the tea came from, the season it was harvested and the finishing style used.

Many of China's finest teas are still made by hand and the skills needed for their manufacture are passed down from one generation to another. Today, more and more people around the world are beginning to appreciate the superb quality and fascinating histories of the vast array of white, yellow, green, black, oolong, puerh, compressed and scented teas that are now more widely available.

Because of restrictions of space, it has only been possible to include a small selection of teas from China. There are many more fascinating varieties available today.

White teas

Baihao Yinzhen (Yinfeng, Silver Needle White Fur)

Character
Produced in Fujian province, this exquisite tea is made only from new buds that are picked before they start to open. 'Baihao' (pek-ho) refers to the tiny white hairs on the underside of each tightly curled leaf bud and which give the tea its beautiful silvery velvet appearance. Yinzhen is picked for only a few days each spring and is sometimes also referred to as Silver Needle White Fur, or Yinfeng. The neatly pointed silver buds stand upright in the water to give a pale yellow liquor that is smooth, sweet and extremely elegant.

Brewing Tips
Brew 5g (0.18oz) in 200ml (7fl oz) water at 76°C (170°F) for 2 minutes. Strain and add more water to the leaves for a second infusion. Alternatively, for just one infusion, brew for 6–8 minutes.

Baihao cup

Baihao dry

Baihao wet

Bai Mudan (Pai Mutan, White Peony)

Character

A Fujian white tea, this is made from tightly curled buds picked with two or three tender young leaves. When they have been dried they have the appearance of little bunches of silver white blossoms (the silver leaf bud) set amongst lightly curled green and pale brown leaves. The leaves are a combination of tips, broken leaf and larger unbroken leaf in colours that range from white to dark green and ochre. The clear, very pale yellow infusion has a sweet muscatel aroma and a velvet smooth, sweet and mild flavour with a hint of nuttiness.

Brewing Tips

This can be brewed either as a green tea, an oolong or even as a black tea, depending on the temperature of the water you choose and the length of time the leaves are steeped. Infuse 4–5g (0.14–0.18oz) in 200ml (7fl oz) water at 93°C (200°F) for 1½–2 minutes. Strain and add more water for a second infusion. Alternatively, for one infusion, steep for 6–7 minutes.

Bai Mudan cup

Bai Mudan dry

Bai Mudan wet

Jade Lily

Character
Tiny fresh buds are intricately hand-tied into delicate, silvery little knots before drying and recall the fascinating handiwork of a skilled lace maker or needlewoman. Brew in a tall glass and watch the underwater ballet as the individual teas absorb water, reveal the amazing neatness of each knot, and sink gracefully to the bottom of the glass to settle with the fattened buds pointing to the surface like little sea creatures. The liquor is like a pale white wine and has a mild, sweet aroma and flavour with undertones of ripe pears.

Brewing Tips
Brew 20 or so knots in a tall glass of 200ml (7fl oz) of hot water at 75°C (167°F) for 4 minutes. Add more water for several infusions.

Jade Lily cup

Jade Lily dry

Jade Lily wet

White Plum

Character
An overwhelmingly beautiful white
tea made from very young leaves that
are skilfully tied by hand into delicate
silvery-gold, six-petalled flowers. Brew
in a tall glass to enjoy the visual
beauty of the flowers absorbing water
to plump out the petals, gradually
floating downwards in the water and
giving out their pale, delicate liquor
and soft, enticing aroma and flavour.

White Plum cup

Brewing Tips
Brew about 10–12 blossoms in
200ml (7fl oz) of hot water at 75°C
(167°F) for 4 minutes. Add more
water for several infusions.

White Plum dry

White Plum wet

Yellow teas

Huangshan Maofeng (Yellow Mountain Hair Peak)

The legend of this tea tells how a beautiful young tea picker was in love with a young man from the same village but the local tyrant kidnapped her to make her his concubine. She managed to escape but discovered that the tyrant had killed her lover and she found his body hidden deep in the mountains. She wept so much over the body that her tears became like rain and turned him into a tea bush. Grown on the mist-covered Huang Mountain in Anhui province, the tea bushes grow amongst wild peach trees.

Huangshan Maofeng cup

Character
This small-leafed yellow tea is made from one leaf and one silvery bud and the dry leaf has a faintly herbal note. As it brews, it gives a very pale yellow liquor that has a rich peachy aroma and a uniquely rich, fruity, slightly nutty flavour.

Huangshan Maofeng dry

Brewing Tips
Brew 5g (0.18oz) in 200ml (7fl oz) water at 82°C (180°F) and infuse for 2 minutes. Strain and add more water for two further infusions.

Huangshan Maofeng wet

Jun Shan Yin Zhen (Jun Mountains Silver Needle)

Character
Silver Needle consists of only the very young, silvery, down-covered buds that are harvested in early spring. The white bushes of northern Fujian province were domesticated from wild tea trees and exhibit silvery down-covered leaves that have been prized for their medicinal properties for more than 1,000 years. The buds stand upright when brewing and give a pale yellow infusion with a buttery texture and a mild aroma.

Jun Shan Yin Zhen cup

Brewing Tips
Brew 5g (0.18oz) in 225ml (8fl oz) water at 76°C (170°F) for 2 minutes. Strain and add more water to the leaves for a second and third infusion.

Jun Shan Yin Zhen dry

Jun Shan Yin Zhen wet

Green teas

Anji White Virgin (despite its name, this is a green tea)

Character
Despite its name, this is a rare
green tea grown in a virgin pure,
pollution-free environment in
Zhejiang province. The silvery-
pale underside of the leaves
and buds account for its name
and it is particularly high in
amino-acids and so is well
respected for its health benefits.
The liquor is very pale, with a
wonderfully sweet flavour and a
hint of astringency.

Brewing Tips
Brew 2.5g (0.09oz) in 200ml
(7fl oz) water at 75°C (167°F) for
2 minutes. Strain and add more
water for another infusion.

Anji White Virgin cup

Anji White Virgin dry

Anji White Virgin wet

Biluochun (Pi Lo Chun, Green Snail Spring)

Character
This famous tea comes from two mountains in Jiangsu province known as East and West Dongting. The bushes grow in very humid conditions surrounded by fruit trees and so absorb the aroma of the blossoms in early spring when the tender leaves of the tea bush are just beginning to form. One new bud and one leaf are plucked and processed by hand into neat little spirals that look like tiny snails. The curled leaves are covered in fine white hairs and untwist to give a clear, green to pale golden-yellow liquor that has a wonderfully delicate and fragrant aroma and a clean aromatic flavour.

Brewing Tips
Brew 5g (0.18oz) in 225ml (8fl oz) water at 76°C (170°F) for 2 minutes. Strain and add more water to the leaves for a second and third infusion.

Biluochun cup

Biluochun dry

Biluochun wet

Jade Rings

Character
These rings are made in Guanshan by meticulously hand-rolling silvery-white, green tea shoots into small rings. When infused, the little rings open up to create a magnificent cup of tea. The flavour from these early spring buds is subtle, sweet and classic.

Brewing Tips
Infuse 5g (0.18oz) in 225ml (8fl oz) water at 82°C (180°F) for 1–2 minutes.

Jade Rings cup

Jade Rings dry

Jade Rings wet

Longjing (Lung Ching, Dragon Well)

This tea is named after the village where it grows in Zhejiang province. The best grade is made from one new bud and one new leaf, which are pressed flat and dried. The next grade, Queshe Longjing (Sparrow's Tongue), is made with a bud and two new leaves which open during brewing to look like a bird's beak and tongue. The teas are famous for their beautiful green colour, elegant shape, smooth flavour and fine aroma.

Longjing cup

Character
The buds point upwards while brewing and release a clear, light yellow-green colour. The clean well-balanced aroma suggests freshly cut grass and toasted chestnuts. The flavour is mellow with a bittersweet-savoury finish.

Brewing Tips
Brew 3g (0.10oz) in 200ml (7fl oz) water at 82°C (180°F) for 2–3 minutes. Strain and add more water for more infusions.

Longjing dry

Longjing wet

Mao Jian

Character

Mao Jian is produced among the misty mountains of Zhejiang, Anhui and Henan provinces and literally translates as 'hairy tip' or 'fur tip'. This is from Zhejiang and has a bright, fresh, clean and rounded character that is refreshing and suits any mood at any time of the day. The long, neat twists of dark, seaweed-green leaf give a vivid, pale lime-green liquor with a complex, slightly sappy aroma and a brisk clean taste that combines dry grass back notes and sweeter floral tones in the foreground.

Brewing Tips

Brew 3g (0.10oz) in 250ml (8.5fl oz) water at 70°C (158°F) for 3 minutes. Add more water for a second infusion.

Mao Jian cup

Mao Jian dry

Mao Jian wet

Tai Ping Huo Kui (Tai Ping Monkey King)

De-enzyming machine in use in China.

Character

High up in the topmost peaks of mountains of Anhui province, each family in Tai Ping Village makes approximately 10 kilos (22 lb) of this famous tea each day during the growing season. After pan-frying, each green leaf is rolled flat between two layers of wire mesh and then fired. This simple method of manufacture captures all the fresh sweetness of the leaf. When brewed, the long, flat, elegant green leaves yield a pale yellow liquor that has a mild, sweet and subtle character with an enticing orchid aroma.

Brewing Tips

Brew 2.5–3g (0.09–0.10oz) in 200ml (7fl oz) water at 75°C (167°F) for 2 minutes. Strain and add more water for a second infusion.

Tai Ping Huo Kui cup

Tai Ping Huo Kui wet

Tai Ping Huo Kui dry

Tian Mu Yun Lo

Character
Close to the natural beauty of West Lake in Zhejiang province, the mountain of Tian Mu (which translates as 'heaven and eyes' or 'eyes looking heavenward') is renowned for its clean pure air and pollution-free environment. 'Yun' means cloud and 'lo' means snail and the tea is so named because of the misty conditions in which the bushes grow and the curly, snail-shell shape of the finished leaf. The tiny, jade green, tender leaves and buds yield a sweet and fragrant liquor.

Brewing Tips
Brew 2.5–3g (0.09–0.10oz) in 200ml (7fl oz) water at 75°C (167°F) for 2 minutes. Strain and add more water for a second infusion.

Tian Mu Yun Lo cup

Tian Mu Yun Lo dry

Tian Mu Yun Lo wet

Yellow Meadow (Huang Tian)

Character
This little-known green tea is manufactured by master tea makers in the small village of Yellow Meadow in Fujian province. The leaf is textured and twisty, dark olive green with yellow-golden flecks and the liquor is pale golden and the flavour and aroma deliciously sweet and aromatic, refreshing and light.

Brewing Tips
Brew 2.5–3g (0.09–0.10oz) in 200ml (7fl oz) water at 80°C (176°F) for 2 minutes. Strain and add more water for two more infusions.

Yellow Meadow cup

Yellow Meadow dry

Yellow Meadow wet

Young Hyson (Flourishing Spring, Lucky Dragon)

Character

As its name indicates, this is made from young leaves gathered in the early spring before the first rains fall. The leaves are twisted into long, thin strips and yield a golden-yellow liquor that has a smooth robust flavour and a pungent aftertaste.

Brewing Tips

Infuse 2.5g (0.09oz) in 200ml (7fl oz) water at 76°C (170°F) for 2 minutes.

Young Hyson cup

Young Hyson dry

Young Hyson wet

Zhen Mei (Chun Mei, Chunmee, Precious Eyebrows)

Character
It is the curved shape of the dried leaves that gives this tea its name. The manufacturing process demands great skill. Each leaf must be rolled at the correct temperature, for the correct amount of time, to achieve the desired curve. The dark jade leaves give a light amber liquor with a soft, smooth, slightly plummy flavour.

Brewing Tips
Brew 2.5g (0.09oz) in 200ml (7fl oz) water at 82°C (180°F) for 3 minutes.

Zhen Mei cup

Zhen Mei dry

Zhen Mei wet

Zu Cha (Pearl Gunpowder)

Most Gunpowder teas are made in Zhejiang province and get their name from the fact that the tightly rolled little 'pearls' of tea look like pellets of gunpowder. Pearl Gunpowder is sold in various sizes from very small 'Pinhead' to larger, more loosely rolled varieties. It was originally marketed in Europe as 'Green Pearl' tea.

Character
The little pellets gradually open in hot water to release their warm amber colour and to give a mellow, quite strong, slightly astringent flavour with a lasting aftertaste.

Brewing Tips
Brew 4–5g (0.14–0.18oz) in 200ml (7fl oz) water at 87°C (190°F) for 2 minutes. Add more water for a second and third infusion.

Zu Cha cup

Zu Cha dry

Zu Cha wet

Gunpowder Tribute (Hui Bai)

Character
Records exist of the manufacture of gunpowder teas in Pingshui city in eastern Zhejiang province during the Tang Dynasty (618–907 AD) and the best of those early teas were given as a tribute to the Chinese emperors. This top grade is made from very young, tender leaves which are lightly rolled into loose grey-green pellets which slowly open to yield a pale yellow liquor that has an exceptional aroma and a pleasing, mouth-filling, sweetly herbal intensity.

Brewing Tips
Brew 2.5g (0.09oz) in 200ml (7fl oz) water at 80°C (176°F) for 3 minutes. Strain and add more water for two more infusions.

Gunpowder Tribute cup

Treasure Teas

These captivating display teas have carefully wrapped dried flowers inside an outer layer of hand-sewn green tea leaves. As the teas slowly absorb water and gracefully unfold, lilies, jasmine flowers, tiny plum blossoms, golden marigolds or amaranth elegantly float from their nest to fill a glass tea pot with colour, perfume and visual beauty. Usually made with small green tea buds and baby leaves, many different and ingenious varieties are now available and have stolen the hearts of tea aficionados everywhere. Brew them in a tall glass or pretty glass teapot for decoration. Alternatively, drink and enjoy the meditative charm of their slow, almost magical revelation.

Flavoured Green Teas

Eight Treasures Tea (Ba Bao Cha)

Character
A traditional favourite from Yunnan province, the blend usually includes green or green jasmine tea, dried wolfberries, sesame seeds, raisins, walnuts, longan, dates and rock sugar. It is said to lower body heat, reduce fatigue, help the digestion and increase appetite. It usually comes in little sachets. The liquor has a fruity, layered aroma and a clean, satisfying, thirst-quenching, energising flavour.

Brewing Tips
Brew one sachet in boiling water for 3 minutes. Add more water for two or more infusions.

Eight Treasures cup

Eight Treasures dry

Eight Treasures wet

Jasmine Pearl

Jasmine teas are produced in Fujian, Jiangsu, Anhui, Hubei, Zhejiang and Sichuan provinces according to tea-scenting techniques that date back more than 900 years. They come as loose-leaf teas and as different-sized spheres. This 'pearl' tea is made by tightly rolling fine, tender, green leaves and buds which are then infused with the essence of fresh jasmine blossoms. After scenting, the jasmine flowers are removed, leaving only the jasmine-scented tea pearls.

Jasmine Pearl cup

Character
The little pearls of tea open up during brewing to release their pale greeny-yellow colour in the water and give a powerful heady aroma of jasmine flowers. The flavour is sweet, smooth, clean and beautifully perfumed.

Brewing Tips
Use a glass or a glass teapot to enjoy the visual beauty of the little pearls opening and floating in the water. Brew 2g (0.07oz) of jasmine pearls in 225ml (8fl oz) water at 87°C (190°F) for 3–4 minutes.

Jasmine Pearl dry

Jasmine Pearl wet

Jasmine Phoenix Eyes

Character
Instead of being rolled into perfect little globes like Jasmine pearls, this exquisite Jasmine is formed from the youngest leaf tips into eye-shaped ovals that are scented eight to ten times with fresh jasmine blossoms. As they slowly open in hot water, they give a head-spinning perfume and have a sweet, jasmine-flavoured liquor that is subtle and delicate, clean and uplifting.

Jasmine Phoenix cup

Brewing Tips
Brew 12–14 eyes in 200ml (7fl oz) water at 80°C (176°F) for 3–4 minutes. Add more water for several further infusions.

Jasmine Phoenix dry

Jasmine Phoenix wet

Moli Huacha (Jasmine)

Jasmine teas are traditionally made by scenting green tea with fresh jasmine flowers. The flowers are picked during the day but stored until the evening when they open to release their heady perfume. The tea is heaped with the flowerheads to allow absorption of the perfume. After several hours, when the heat produced by the tea begins to increase, the flowers are removed and the tea is layered with fresh flowers. This is repeated several times.

Moli Huacha cup

Character
Loose, lightly fermented pouchong leaves mixed with delicate dried jasmine petals infuse to give a pale amber liquor that has a powerfully perfumed aroma and flavour.

Moli Huacha dry

Brewing Tips
Brew 3.5g (0.12oz) in 200ml (7fl oz) water at 87°C (190°F) for 2 minutes. Strain and add more water for two further infusions.

Moli Huacha wet

Oolong teas

Phoenix Supreme Oolong

Hand-picked from bushes that grow on the Wudong peak of Phoenix Mountain in Guangdong province, this tea is made in small batches by experienced tea masters. The leaves are gathered twice a year (in April–May and October–November), when they are half-open, and processed by the special Phoenix method of 'rattling' the leaves and partial oxidation that lasts for 8–10 hours.

Phoenix Supreme cup

Character
The greeny-brown leaves are tightly twisted fine strips. The light-golden clear liquor has a fragrant fruity aroma and a smooth, very refreshing flavour.

Phoenix Supreme dry

Brewing Tips
Brew 3–4g (0.10–0.14oz) in 150ml (5fl oz) water at 85°C (185°F) for 1 minute 15 seconds. Strain and add more water for one further infusion.

Phoenix Supreme wet

Qing Xiang Dan Cong (Pure Fragrance Oolong)

Character
A medium, oxidized, oolong tea that yields an exhilarating aroma and complex, multilayered infusion with a unique pear element.

Brewing Tips
Brew 5g (0.18oz) in 200ml (7fl oz) water at 87°C (180°F) for 15 minutes. Strain and add more water for three further infusions.

Qing Xiang Dan Cong cup

Qing Xiang Dan Cong dry

Qing Xiang Dan Cong wet

Ro Gui

Character
Also known as 'Cassia Oolong', 'Wuyi
Cassia Oolong', and 'Cassia Bark',
this is another of Fujian province's
famous 'rock' oolongs. The dark,
greeny-brown, lightly curled, long
leaves sometimes carry the subtly
sweet and spicy aroma of cassia, a
cinnamon-like bark. The liquor is
very clear, golden amber which has a
honey, orchid aroma and a full, rich,
very slightly smoky flavour with a
lingering citrus aftertaste.

Brewing Tips
Brew 3–4g (0.10–0.14oz) in 200ml
(7fl oz) of near boiling water for 1–2
minutes. Strain and add more water
for eight further infusions.

Ro Gui cup

Ro Gui dry

Ro Gui wet

Ti Kuan Yin (Tieguanyin, Tea of the Iron Goddess of Mercy)

Probably the best known of Chinese oolongs, this aromatic and elegant tea comes from central Fujian province. Its legend tells how a tea grower in the area would walk past an iron statue of Kuan Yin, the Goddess of Mercy, on his way to work each day. The statue stood in a small temple that was rather dilapidated and, although he could not afford to actually repair the building, the tea grower started to take care of it, cleaning it and lighting incense. Then one night, in a dream, the goddess told him to look in a cave behind the temple for a treasure that was hidden there. When he looked the next day he found a single tea shoot which he nurtured and cultivated. He named the tea Ti Kuan Yin.

Ti Kuan Yin cup

Ti Kuan Yin dry

Character
The crinkly, slightly twisted leaves are a mixture of reddy-brown and dark green and as they brew, they unfurl to give lace-edged leaves that release a honey-coloured liquor, a sweet, floral aroma and an orchid-like, smooth, delicate flavour.

Brewing Tips
Brew 3.5g (0.12oz) in 200ml (7 fl oz) water at 95°C (200 F) for 1.5–2 minutes. Add more water for two or three further infusions.

Ti Kuan Yin wet

Flavoured oolongs

Ginseng Oolong

Character
Lightly oxidised oolong is blended with powdered ginseng to give dense olive-green pellets that brew to yield a pleasing floral aroma and a surprising, sweet taste. Ginseng is thought to stimulate the mind and the body and this increasingly popular oolong is refreshing, revitalising and uplifting.

Brewing Tips
Brew 2.5–3g (0.09–0.10oz) in 200ml (7fl oz) water at 85°C (185°F) for 2 minutes. Strain and add more water for three further infusions.

Ginseng Oolong cup

Ginseng Oolong dry

Ginseng Oolong wet

Osmanthus Oolong

Character
Delicate, tiny golden trumpets of
osmanthus blossoms are dried and
blended with green, 30 per cent
oxidised Tie Kuan Yin to give a
wonderful, aromatic infusion that fills
the mouth with sweet, silky, perfumed
magic and heady floral perfume.

Brewing Tips
Brew 2.5g (0.09oz) in 200ml (7fl oz)
water at 80°C (176°F) for 2 minutes.
Strain and add more water for two or
more further infusions.

Osmanthus Oolong cup

Osmanthus Oolong dry

Osmanthus Oolong wet

Black Teas

Pang Yang Gong Fu (Golden Monkey Black Tea)

Character
Visually stunning, long, twisted dry
leaf mingles with velvety, taupe-gold
buds and yields a clear, honey-brown
liquor that carries the aroma of
glowing, lightly smoking embers and
has a satisfying, slightly smoky taste
with hints of drying hay and lingering
notes of apricots.

Brewing Tips
Brew 2.5g (0.09oz) in 200ml (7fl oz)
of boiling water for 3 minutes.

Pang Yang Gong Fu cup

Pang Yang Gong Fu dry

Pang Yang Gong Fu wet

Qimen Hao Ya (Keemun Downy Bud)

Character
This shiny black tea is named after the area where it is produced – Qimen in Anhui province – and is considered to be among the elite of Chinese teas. Keemuns come in different grades but all have a similar jet-black appearance and are often used as a quality, well-balanced base for flavoured teas. The tightly twisted, slender jet-black leaves give a rich coppery brew that has a sweet floral aroma and a satisfyingly rich, winey flavour.

Brewing Tips
Brew 2.5g (0.09oz) in 200ml (7fl oz) water at 100°C (212°F) for 3 minutes. Add more water for a second and third infusion.

Qimen Hao Ya cup

Qimen Hao Ya dry

Qimen Hao Ya wet

Yunnan Gold

Character
Yunnan province has been producing teas for more than 1,700 years. The black teas from this region are made from the leaves of the local broad-leafed variety of the tea bush and the tea displays big golden buds and uniform-shaped leaves. The black leaves have a generous scattering of golden buds and brew to give a liquor that is a rich, dark reddish-black with a molasses-like sweetness and malty finish.

Brewing Tips
Brew 2.5g (0.09oz) in 225ml (8fl oz) water at 100 °C (212 °F) for 3–4 minutes.

Yunnan Gold cup

Yunnan Gold dry

Yunnan Gold wet

Wuyi Lapsang (Bohea Lapsang)

Character

In the Wuyi mountains of Fujian province, the large tea-drying ovens of the local factories have, for centuries, been fired by pine logs chopped and gathered in the surrounding forests. As the hot, slightly smoky air rises through vents in the ceiling into the drying room above, the tea absorbs hints of the smouldering wood and develops the characteristic hint of lingering smokiness. The peat-black, large twists of leaf give a beautiful, hazel-gold liquor with golden hues, the aroma of warm pine, an exquisitely smooth, gently smoky flavour and a creamy liquorice-root aftertaste.

Brewing Tips

Brew 2.5g (0.09oz) in 200ml (7fl oz) of boiling water for 4–5 minutes.

Wuyi Lapsang cup

Wuyi Lapsang dry

Wuyi Lapsang wet

Zengshan Xiaozhong (Lapsang Souchong, Smoked Tea)

Character

Lapsang Souchong teas are a speciality of Fujian province. Souchong means 'sub-variety' and refers to the type of tea bush that grows in the Wuyi Mountains. The leaves are withered over pine or cypress wood fires and then pan-fried and rolled. Next they are pressed into wooden barrels, covered with a cloth and left to oxidize. Then the leaves are fried and rolled into tight strips. Finally, they are hung in baskets over smoking pine wood fires to dry. The intensely black leaves give a dark red liquor that has a distinctive smoky aroma and flavour.

Brewing Tips

Brew 2.5g (0.09oz) in 200ml (7fl oz) water at 100°C (212°F) for 3–4 minutes. Strain and add more water to the leaves for a second and third infusion.

Zengshan Xiaozhong cup

Zengshan Xiaozhong dry

Zengshan Xiaozhong wet

Hand-tied Black Teas

Dragon Whiskers

Character

From Anhui province, this tea is aptly named for its bundles of black leaves that are bound together in colourful silk threads. This is also available as a green tea. The dark twisted leaves and furry tips yield a golden infusion that has a robust aroma and a sweet nutty flavour with a long smooth finish.

Brewing Tips

Pull the end of the thread and unwind from around the leaves. Brew one piece in 225ml (8fl oz) water at 100°C (212°F) for 3 minutes. Add more water for two further infusions.

Dragon Whiskers dry

Hong Mudan (Black Sea Anemone)

Character

This black, display tea is made in southern Anhui province on a remote mountain where virtually every family grows tea. The 'anemones' are made from quality, spring-picked leaves that are then tied into beautiful rosettes. The tea is meant to be enjoyed for its visual appeal as well as for its fragrance and flavour. As it brews, the rosette unfurls to resemble a sea anemone. The fragrance and flavour are sweet and delicate.

Brewing Tips

Brew one rosette in a glass of 225ml (8fl oz) water at 85°C (185°F) for several minutes to allow the rosette to gradually bloom. Add more water as required and the rosette will continue to give colour and flavour without becoming bitter.

Hong Mudan dry

Red Tower

Character
Exquisitely hand-crafted in Fujian
province, the leaf of these little pointy
cones of tea combine black-brown
leaf with burnished copper, orange
and gold strands that gradually open
in boiling water to give an aroma that
hints at roasting sweet potatoes and a
smooth, sweet taste that hints at
treacle and warm oiled wood.

Brewing Tips
Brew three towers in 200ml (7fl oz)
of boiling water for 3–4 minutes.
Strain and add more water for two or
more further infusions.

Red Tower cup

Red Tower dry

Red Tower wet

Flavoured Black Teas

Lanhsiang (Lanxiang) Orchid Scented

Most of China's flavoured and
scented teas are made from green
leaves, but some oolongs and blacks
are also blended with flower
fragrances. Orchid-scented teas are
perfumed with flowers of
Chloranthus Spicatus.

Character
Neat browny-black leaves give an
amber liquor that has a sweetly
perfumed aroma and an exotic and
luxurious flavour.

Brewing Tips
Infuse 2.5g (0.09oz) in 200ml (7fl oz)
water at 87°C (200°F) for 1–2
minutes. Strain and add more water
for one or two further infusions.

Lanhsiang cup

Lanhsiang dry

Lanhsiang wet

Meigui Hongcha (Rose Congou, Rose Petal Black)

Character
'Congou' comes from the Chinese word *Kungfu*, which has to do with skill and dedicated learning. Congou teas all consist of carefully made, neat, unbroken black leaf. Rose Congou is blended with dried pink rose petals to give a powerfully fragrant aroma and a warm coppery infusion that is smooth, mellow and gently flavoured with sweet roses.

Brewing Tips
Brew 2.5g (0.09oz) in 200ml (7fl oz) water at 100°C (212°F) for 3–4 minutes. Strain and add more water for one or two further infusions.

Meigui Hongcha cup

Meigui Hongcha dry

Meigui Hongcha wet

Lychee Red Black

Character
From Guangdong province, the dry,
dark brown, woody leaf fills the air
with a powerful sweet, fruity perfume
that absolutely replicates the aroma
from fresh lychees as the outer shell
of each fruit is carefully peeled back.
The liquor is rich copper in colour
and syrupy sweet and fruity in aroma
and taste. Deliciously uplifting!

Brewing Tips
Brew 3g (0.10oz) in approximately
250ml (8$\frac{1}{2}$fl oz) boiling water for 3–4
minutes. Strain and add more water
for a second infusion.

Lychee Red Black cup

Lychee Red Black dry

Lychee Red Black wet

Puerh Teas

Raw Puerh Mini Tuo Cha (Xiaguan Factory)

Character

From Xiaguan factory in Yunnan province, this raw puerh gives a vibrantly rich but subtle liquor that breathes hints of smokiness and finishes with the gentle sweetness of apricots and peaches.

Brewing Tips

Place 1–2 mini cakes in a teapot or cup, add near-boiling water and rinse the tea for 4–5 seconds then pour that first water away. Add boiling water and allow to infuse for 2–3 minutes. Strain and add more water for five to six further infusions, allowing less steeping time for each infusion.

Raw Puerh Mini Tuo Cha cup

Raw Puerh Mini Tuo Cha dry

Raw Puerh Mini Tuo Cha wet

Cooked Puerh Mini Tuo Cha (Menghai Factory)

Character
Neat little compressed, ball-shaped cakes of cooked puerh give a dark red liquor and an intensely satisfying, multi-layered, earthy aroma and taste that recalls misty autumn woodland and fallen leaves.

Brewing Tips
Brew 1 mini cake in a teapot or cup in boiling water for 1 minute. Strain and add more water for five to six further infusions, brewing for slightly fewer seconds each time more water is added.

Cooked Puerh Mini Tuo Cha cup

Cooked Puerh Mini Tuo Cha dry

Cooked Puerh Mini Tuo Cha wet

Tuo Cha

Character

This compressed tea is like a very neat round bird's nest. It is made by pressing fermented and steamed puerh leaves into cakes which are then left to age. Tuo cha gives a rich, dark brew that has the typical earthy aroma and flavour of puerh teas.

Brewing Tips

Break off 3-5g (0.10–0.18oz) and steep in 200ml (7fl oz) water at 100°C (212°F) for 10–20 seconds. Separate the liquor from the leaf and add more water for several further infusions.

Tuo Cha Raw Tippy Puerh

Character

Woody twists of leaf mingle amber-gold shades with oaky browns and the dry tea breathes a soft, sweet, appealingly autumnal aroma. The liquor is pale amber with beautiful pink hues and carries smooth, mellow earthiness and suggestions of sweet, damp woodland air.

Raw Tippy Puerh Tuo Cha cup

Brewing Tips

Brew 2.5-3g (0.09–0.10oz) in 200ml (7fl oz) of boiling water for 30–40 seconds. Strain and add more water for six to seven further infusions, allowing approximately 1 minute for each infusion.

Raw Tippy Puerh Tuo Cha dry

Raw Tippy Puerh Tuo Cha wet

Cooked Gold Tip Puerh

Character
From the snowy mountains of North West Yunnan, the fine, twisty, hazel-brown strands of leaf yield a juicy, brown-black liquor that has an earthy aroma that is reminiscent of damp autumn leaves and a silky-sweet flavour with undertones of caramelised figs and a sweet liquorice aftertaste.

Brewing Tips
Brew 3–5g (0.10–0.18oz) in 250ml (8½fl oz) of boiling water for 10–20 seconds. Strain and add more water for five to six further infusions, gradually reducing the amount of steeping time for each infusion.

Cooked Gold Tip Puerh cup

Cooked Gold Tip Puerh dry

Cooked Gold Tip Puerh wet

2000 Wild Raw Puerh Tea Cake 357g

Character

Many of the larger compressed cakes of puerh are too expensive for many people to buy but discs like this outstanding 2000 Yi Wu Mountain Puerh from Xisuanbanna in Southern Yunnan is excellent value and will yield approximately 700 infusions. The deep copper and walnut-coloured dry leaf gives a golden green liquor that has a clean, multi-layered, elegant and nutty aroma and flavour. Further infusions bring a richer, more complex, umami character with darker tones of fern and citrus peel.

Brewing Tips

Brew 4–5g (0.16–0.18oz) in 250ml (8½fl oz) of boiling water for not more than 15–30 seconds. Strain and add more water for seven to eight further infusions.

Puerh cakes are often stacked in sevens for retail. Seven is considered a lucky number in China.

Georgia

Georgia grows tea in the fertile foothills of the snow-capped Caucasus Mountains that form the border between Georgia and Russia. Conditions here are ideal for tea cultivation – clean air, fertile soil, organic farming methods and plenty of rain and clear running water. Tea was first cultivated here in 1890 and because the tea produced was so good, under Russian control the area became the main source of tea for Soviet samovars. New technology was introduced, including mechanical harvesters and factory machines, and the long-term effect was to reduce the quality of Georgian tea. Since independence from

Russia, however, Georgia and the rest of the world are discovering the country's fine and unusual 'hand-made' teas, for, although the outside world knew nothing of their activities, Georgian families have for decades been quietly making black tea by hand in their farmhouses. And now, with the help of British consultant Nigel Melican of Teacraft Ltd and Georgian entrepreneur Tamaz Mikadze, these Georgian teas are finding their way onto the world market.

Since 2003, around 700 families from West Georgia have joined together to form the Tea Producer Farmers' Association – Caucasus Tea.

Members must produce either 'hand-made' tea, made entirely by hand without the use of any machinery at all, or 'village-made tea', made using small-scale, locally designed machinery that in many cases has been made by the village blacksmith. Older members who have been making tea all their lives are passing on their skills and knowledge to the younger generation. The Georgian pluckers generally pick one bud and three leaves and, when the leaves have been carried home, they are withered in a cool room or on a shaded veranda, then rolled by hand by whatever method each family has chosen. In one house, the leaf is rolled in an enamel bowl, in another it is rolled on a flat board that has wires stretched across it. After this vigorous rolling, the leaf is left to oxidize for 4–8 hours, depending on the weather and ambient temperature and is then spread out in full sunlight to dry. At times of the year when there is not enough warm sunlight, the teas can be taken to a factory/quality control centre in a nearby town where the leaf is mechanically dried. The factory is also used as a warehouse for the made teas so that bulk quantities can be consolidated before shipment to customers in the US and UK. Instead of shipping small parcels as the Association members once did, enough hand-made tea is now being produced to fill 20ft containers.

Other tea farmers in Georgia have been working for the past five or six years, with help from Nigel Melican, to produce speciality machine-made teas. In September 2003, local baker, Merab Vasadze, decided to refurbish his disused Kolkhuri tea factory in Makvaneti village in the Ozurgeti region of West Georgia and, having acquired or designed new machinery and equipment, is now making orthodox speciality teas such as Kolkhuri Extra and Kolkhuri Artisan. The teas now rival the character and colour of the hand-made Georgian teas.

Thanks mainly to the involvement of Martin Bauer, German wholesaler, in a green tea venture since the 1990s, Georgia is also now the fourth largest green tea exporter into the European Union.

Tea-maker Natela Gujabidze holding a batch of her hand-made black tea.

Natela's Tea GOPA

The hand-made Georgian black teas are classified and marketed under the name of the person who makes them and one of the most prominent manufacturers is Natela Gujabidze. She has been making tea in her village of Nagobileui in Western Georgia all her life. She makes the tea entirely by hand and the fine long leaves are gently hand-rolled and then dried in the Georgian sunshine.

Natela's Tea GOPA cup

Character
The browny-black, twisted tangle of leaves is flecked with distinct golden tips. The infusion this gives is mid-amber in colour and has a deliciously sweet and mellow flavour with a hint of citrus and chestnut. After brewing, the leaves have the appearance of an oolong, with a rich mix of ruddy brown and dark green.

Brewing Tips
Brew 2.5g (0.09oz) in 200ml (7fl oz) water at 100°C (212°F) for 5 minutes.

Natela's Tea GOPA dry

Natela's Tea GOPA wet

Georgian Old Lady

Character
Another tea plucked and processed by Natela, the hand-rolled tender buds and tips give a dry leaf that is a beautiful mix of dark brown curled leaf and gold wiry flecks. The amber gold liquor has a mild sweetness and velvety smoothness with light fruity undertones.

Brewing Tips
Brew 2.5–3g (0.09–0.10oz) in 200ml (7fl oz) of near-boiling water for 5 minutes.

Georgian Old Lady cup

Georgian Old Lady dry

Georgian Old Lady wet

Ilia's Tea OP1

Ilia Basilashvili makes a 'village-made tea' using finely plucked leaf and a small home-made rolling table and rotary dryer.

Character
The very dark browny-black leaf is rather like a small version of a Yunnan tea in appearance. Some of the pieces of leaf are lightly curved, others straighter. It brews to give a bright, clear, dark amber infusion that has the aroma of honey and is sweet and smooth.

Brewing Tips
Brew 2.5g (0.09oz) in 200ml (7fl oz) water at 100°C (212°F) for 5 minutes.

Kolkhuri Extra

Character
Machine-made by Mereb Vasadze in the Georgian village of Makvaneti, production methods have been steadily improved since 2003 to give attractive, flavoursome teas that match the hand-made Georgian teas. This neat, very black, wiry, broken leaf from the Kolkhuri Ltd tea factory is lightly flecked with tiny, pointed golden tips. It yields a dark amber liquor with a sweet aroma that breathes hints of molten brown sugar and a sweet, slightly flavoursome character with undertones of roasting brazil nuts.

Brewing Tips
Brew 2.5–3g (0.09–0.10oz) in 200ml (7fl oz) of boiling water for 3–4 minutes.

Kolkhuri Extra cup

Kolkhuri Extra dry

Kolkhuri Extra wet

Kolkhuri Artisan

Character
Also made by Mereb Vasadze, this long, twisty whole black leaf from the Kolkhuri factory in Makyaneti gives a crystal clear amber-gold liquor that is full of raisin sweetness and has a smooth, light, liquor with a ripe, vine fruit character.

Brewing tips
Brew 3g (0.10oz) in 200ml (7fl oz) of boiling water for 5 minutes.

Kolkhuri Artisan cup

Kolkhuri Artisan dry

Kolkhuri Artisan wet

India

In the late eighteenth century, the tea plant was discovered growing as a native of Assam and the climate and altitude were declared to be suitable for tea cultivation. But it was not until 1834, after trials with the plant in Calcutta's botanical gardens, that commercial production started. The first plantings were made with seeds of the Chinese plant, *Camellia sinensis*, and these did not thrive. Eventually, it was decided that the local *Camellia sinensis assamica* should be used instead and this enabled the plants to flourish. The first made Assam tea was shipped from India in 1838 and sold at the London Tea Auctions in January 1839 to declarations that it was every bit as good as tea from China. During the 1850s, the tea industry spread northwards up into Darjeeling and Bengal and then to Nilgiri in the beautiful Blue Mountains of India's south-western tip. Production increased rapidly from 183.4 tonnes (180.5 tons) in 1853 to 6,700 tonnes (6,594 tons) in 1870 and 35,274 tonnes (34,716.9 tons) in 1885. By 1947, when India won its independence from Britain, annual tea production stood at 28 million kg (276,650 tons). Since independence, the amount of land under tea has increased by 40 per cent and production has gone up by 250 per cent. Over the five year period from 2007, production is expected to rise by 30–50 per cent, with a Rs 48 billion Special Purpose Tea Fund pledged by

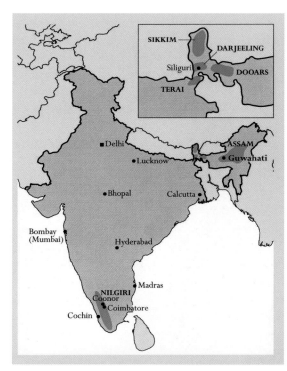

the government to fund the cutting and pruning of old bushes and the replanting of fields where bushes are more than 40 years old. Rejuvenation and replanting is expected to increase both quantity and quality and to attract a good response from overseas buyers.

Today, India is one of the world's largest tea producers, with over 13,000 gardens and a workforce of more than 1.1 million employees who in turn generate income for a further 10 million people. India produces a mixture of orthodox and CTC black teas, many of which in the past were exported to Russia and Britain but which today are mostly consumed domestically. Some manufacturers concentrate on the production of CTC fannings and dust for the export teabag market, while others produce grainy CTC grades specifically for the home market. In 1993, 83 per cent of production was of CTC teas. A small number of planters in the major growing regions still prefer to offer high-quality, large-leaf orthodox teas to the connoisseur market both at home and abroad, and, with a change in markets around the world and a shift in consumer tastes, are now also making green, white and oolong teas as well as the traditional speciality blacks.

The Tea Board of India has worked steadily over the past few years to improve and maintain the reputation of teas from the country's three most important growing areas – Darjeeling, Assam and Nilgiri. Because of their

The tea-covered slopes of Darjeeling, India.

consistently high quality, international demand for these teas has grown over the years and a situation had developed whereby teas were being misleadingly labelled and marketed as 'Pure Assam', 'Pure Darjeeling' and 'Pure Nilgiri', when in fact they were blended with teas from other countries and regions. In recent years, the Tea Board has been keen to ensure that all teas marketed as Assam, Darjeeling or Nilgiri genuinely contain 100 per cent tea from those regions and has introduced a system of distinctive logos which, when displayed on the side of packets or tins, guarantees the genuine article. Teas from packers and blenders are regularly checked and certified by the Tea Board.

Assam

Assam, the 'land of the one-horned rhino', is a vast and beautiful area of dense forests and open rolling plains through which the mighty Brahmaputra river runs, carrying rich fertile soil down from the mountains of Tibet to the agricultural plains that stretch out on either side of the river. This is the largest tea-growing area in the world where, in 1993, almost 450,000 tonnes (442,893 tons) of tea were produced in 2,000 gardens – 53 per cent of the all-India record crop of 835,552.7 tonnes (822,356 tons) and today, Assam tea accounts for 55 per cent of India's total annual production. However, lack of rain in 2006 caused a fall in production and during the first four months of the season, Assam production was down to 59,500 tonnes (58,560 tons) from 64,000 tonnes (62,989 tons) in the corresponding period of 2005. Statistics from the Indian Tea Board indicated that production from the whole of India was down by approximately 6 per cent in 2006 and that Assam was the worst affected.

The Brahmaputra Valley shares borders with China, Burma and Bangladesh and although Assam teas are quite different from Darjeeling teas, the two areas lie only 120 miles apart. The rainfall in Assam is extremely high, usually between 200–300cm (80–120in) per year but sometimes exceeding 10m (33ft) in just one season. In one day, up to 30cm (12in) of rain can fall, making the air heavy with humidity and the ground extremely wet. During the rainy season, the temperatures can rise to 100°C and on the plantations it is rather like being inside a vast glass greenhouse. The plants love these conditions and grow vigorously from spring to late autumn before the winter cold sends the bushes into their annual period of dormancy.

As in other major producing regions of the world, the Assam plantations and research centres have concentrated their efforts on producing cloned tea plants that can withstand drought, flooding, attacks by pests and disease, and which also offer an increased output of leaf. The leaf is made into both orthodox and CTC teas and then sold at the Guwuhati auctions, which mainly sell teas for the domestic market, or at the Siliguri and Calcutta auctions, which offer teas for export.

First Flush Assam

First Flush Tiraputi

When the early spring weather in March brings warmth to the Brahmaputra Valley, the tea bushes begin to push out new leaf shoots and are plucked to make Assam First Flush teas. These are not considered to be the best of Assam tea production and are sold mainly for blending. However, occasionally a good First Flush will be offered as a single source speciality tea and usually has a rich and fresh aroma and flavour, though not the full malty depth of a Second Flush.

Character
This tippy tea produces a mellow, caramel-coloured tea with a long smooth finish. It drinks well with milk.

Brewing Tips
Infuse 2.5g (0.09oz) in 200ml (7fl oz) water at 100°C (212°F) for 3–4 minutes.

First Flush Tiraputi cup

First Flush Tiraputi dry

First Flush Tiraputi wet

Second Flush Assam

Harmutty

The plucking of tea to make Second Flush Assams begins in June and continues through to September. The dry leaf of Second Flush Assams is characteristically a rich warm brown in colour with a good proportion of golden flecks mixed through it. These are the very tips of the new leaves, so new when picked that they do not contain the same proportion of tea chemicals as slightly larger leaves and so do not darken during the oxidation and drying period. The high level of tippy leaves shows a carefully made, good-quality Assam tea. When the teas are brewed they give a warm coppery-coloured liquor and a rich, smooth, slightly sweet maltiness – a taste that is a favourite first thing in the morning and at breakfast.

Harmutty cup

Character
Large pieces of well-sorted tippy leaf that are a warm brown colour and flecked throughout with beautiful golden tips. The infusion is a wonderful mid-amber colour and the flavour is rich, sweet, malty and exquisitely smooth.

Harmutty dry

Brewing Tips
Brew 2.5g (0.09 oz) in 200ml (7fl oz) water at 100°C (212°F) for 4–5 minutes.

Harmutty wet

Assam Green

Fatikchera

With a growing interest in green teas around the world, various regions of India are producing more and more green varieties. Assam greens tend to be light and delicate and have a slightly sweet aroma and flavour.

Brewing Tips
Brew 2.5g (0.09 oz) in 200ml (7fl oz) water at 85°C (185°F) for 2–3 minutes.

Character
Long fine pieces of green leaf that display a mixture of colours from pale jade to dark olive-brown. The pale amber infusion has a slightly grassy aroma and a lightly astringent flavour with citrus overtones.

Fatikchera dry

Assam White

Satrupa

Character
Satrupa Estate is located on the banks of the Buri-Dihing river in Upper Assam, about a day's journey away from the Burmese border. The liquor from the beautiful needle-like leaf has a fruity, floral aroma and the taste is reminiscent of fresh cucumber, butternut squash and melons.

Brewing Tips
Brew 2.5g (0.09oz) in 200ml (7fl oz) water at 75°C (167°F) for 3 minutes. Drain, add more water and steep for 7–9 minutes for a second and third infusion.

Satrupa cup

Darjeeling

The little hill town of Darjeeling nestles among the foothills of the snowcapped Himalayan mountains in the north-eastern corner of India. Commercial cultivation began here in the 1850s, when gardens were established at Tukvar, Aloobari and Steinthal. By 1866, there were 39 gardens producing 21,000 kg (46,300lbs) of tea. By 1874 there were 113 gardens, with 6,000 hectares (14,800 acres) under tea.

Today, Darjeeling has 86 gardens planted out over an area of 19,000 hectares (47,000 acres) that produce over 10 million kg (2.2 million lb) every year. On the higher slopes, where altitudes reach 2,135 metres (7,000 feet), the Chinese variety of the tea plant is grown, since it withstands the intensely cold winters and the cool summer nights better than the Assam variety. But on the lower slopes, at altitudes of 915 metres (3,000 feet), *Camellia sinensis assamica* grows quite happily in temperatures that are a little less harsh and where the air is a little more gentle. The unusual combination of high mountains, steep terrain, well-drained soil, extreme cold in winter and intense heat in summer, misty swirling clouds, a good level of well-distributed rainfall and pure, clean mountain air produces the exquisite muscatel character and flowery aroma of good Darjeelings, which earns them the title, 'champagne' of Indian teas. Because of the changing seasons, tea bushes in this part of India do not grow all year round. The bush is dormant from late November to early March; when the first rains have fallen and the first spring sunshine warmed the air, the bushes start growing again. The first new shoots, the First Flush, are picked during late March and April and produce teas that benefit from all the flavour and intensity stored in the bushes through the winter months. The Second Flush is picked in May and June. These teas have all the character of First Flush but tend to be more developed. The monsoon arrives in mid-June and drenches the area with roughly 3m (10ft) of rain before September brings a drier season. Teas that grow during the monsoon period contain a high proportion of water; they have the familiar character of Darjeeling teas but are less spectacular in flavour and aroma. Leaves that are gathered in the autumn months give a more mature flavour but are still aromatic and reminiscent of muscatel grapes.

First Flush Darjeeling

Goomtee

First Flush Darjeelings are usually fresh, flowery, puckery, light and extremely aromatic. They are much sought after on world markets, win prizes at speciality food and drink events and fetch very high prices at auction – sometimes more than £290 (570 US$) per kilo. Because of the variations in quality and character of teas from individual plantations each year, First Flush Darjeelings are sometimes treated rather like Beaujolais Nouveau and are flown in early, ahead of the normal shipments, for eager customers impatient to try the new season's teas. Many retailers now appreciate the fact that discerning customers enjoy making the comparison between Darjeelings from different gardens and different seasons and so sell a range of teas from named gardens and specific harvests.

Goomtee is ranked each year among the top gardens in Darjeeling, along with Jungpana, Poobong, Thurbo, Castelton, Selimbong, Chamong and Margaret's Hope.

Character
Very green leaf showing colours ranging from bright light green to dark olive and oaky brown. The liquor is a pale greeny-amber colour, and has a deliciously sweet muscatel flavour with traditional winey overtones.

Brewing Tips
Brew 2.5g (0.09oz) in 200ml (7fl oz) water at 82°C (180°F) for 3 minutes.

Goomtee cup

Goomtee dry

Goomtee wet

Second Flush Darjeeling

Tong Song

Second Flush Darjeelings are made from teas plucked in May and June. Since the bushes have been steadily strengthening as the year progresses, the flavour of the teas is slightly more developed than that of First Flush teas. Many people prefer the slightly more mature character of these teas and consider them the best that Darjeeling produces.

Character
Mainly brown leaf mingled with hints of olive green and gold to give a pale amber cup with a sweet honey-like flavour.

Brewing Tips
Brew 2.5g (0.09 oz) in 200ml (7fl oz) water at 100°C (212°F) for 3 minutes.

Tong Song cup

Tong Song dry

Tong Song wet

Darjeeling Autumnal

Oaks

During the monsoon summer months the heavy rains give teas that are of a more ordinary quality and character than First and Second Flush. Then, in the autumn, after the monsoon, come the autumnal teas. The autumnals have the Darjeeling character but give a darker, amber-coloured liquor that has a smoother, more rounded, mature flavour and a little more body compared to the teas made earlier in the year.

Character
Mixed colour leaf displaying pieces that are bright green through to deep jade and brown. The infusion is greeny-brown and has a pronounced sweet muscatel aroma and a gentle, lightly fruity flavour.

Brewing Tips
Brew 2.5g (0.09oz) in 200ml (7fl oz) water at 100°C (212°F) for 3–4 minutes.

Darjeeling Autumnal Oaks cup

Darjeeling Autumnal Oaks dry

Darjeeling Autumnal Oaks wet

Darjeeling White

Poobong

Character
A bud and two new leaves are picked to make a tea that looks similar to Chinese Bai Mudan. The buds remain silvery while the surrounding leaves are a mixture of sage green and brown. The infusion is pale greeny-yellow, the aroma has a hint of lemon and the flavour is very light and slightly citrus.

Brewing Tips
Brew 2.5g (0.09 oz) in 200ml (7fl oz) water at 85°C (180°F) for 5–6 minutes.

Poobong cup

Poobong dry

Poobong wet

Darjeeling Green

Selim Hill

Character
Large, slightly twisted, dark greeny-brown leaf. The jade green infusion has an aroma that reminds you of the seashore and the lightly astringent, herby flavour is round and full in the mouth.

Brewing Tips
Brew 2.5g (0.09 oz) in 200ml (7fl oz) water at 85°C (180°F) for 2–3 minutes.

Selim Hill dry

Darjeeling Oolong

Goomtee

Character
Young Darjeeling leaves and buds are semi-oxidized to give a beautiful, curled oaky brown dry leaf flecked with silvery buds and tips. The light copper-coloured liquor is a smooth, sweet infusion with aromatic, fruity tones and lingering floral notes.

Brewing Tips
Brew 2.5g (0.09oz) in 200ml (7fl oz) water at 90°C (194°F) for 4–5 minutes. Strain and add more water for further infusions.

Darjeeling Oolong Goomtee cup

Darjeeling Oolong Goomtee dry

Darjeeling Oolong Goomtee wet

Dooars

Kamala

Tea production started in the Dooars region in the 1860s in a small area lying amongst the Himalayan foothills, just west of Assam and just south of Darjeeling, where little hill streams run down through the tea plantations that cover the gently sloping hillsides all around. The teas grown here are typically dark and full-bodied but have less character than Assam teas.

Character
The leaf of this typical orthodox Dooars tea is a mixture of pale sage green and pale golden-brown. The infusion is the colour of whisky and has a light flavour with a hint of astringency.

Brewing Tips
Brew 2.5g (0.09oz) in 200ml (7fl oz) water at 100°C (212°F) for 3–4 minutes.

Nilgiri

Some 1,500 miles south of Darjeeling and Assam, India's southern tea plantations stretch through the range of the Nilgiri Hills or 'Blue Mountains' that run down the south-western tip of the country from Kerala to Tamil Nadu. In 1840, the first British planter, Colonel John Ouchterlony, and his brother James decided to establish tea plantations in the midst of stunningly beautiful, rolling grasslands and dense jungles where eucalyptus trees, cypresses and blue gum trees grow and elephants roam free. With its high elevations and approximately 200cm (80in) of rainfall every year, Nilgiri is an extremely suitable location and today there are roughly 25,000 hectares (62,000 acres) of land under tea, growing at altitudes of between 300 and 1,800m (1,000 and 6,000ft) above sea level. Every slope, valley and plateau is covered with tea bushes that grow steadily throughout the year. Although the new shoots are plucked all year, the two most important harvesting periods are in April and May, when approximately 25 per cent of the crop is picked, and again from September to December, when a further 35 to 40 per cent of the annual crop is gathered. The black teas produced here are flavourful, bright and brisk, often with a similar character to the Ceylon teas that grow to the east on the island of Sri Lanka. The majority of these teas are used in blending but more and more are now marketed as single source teas. Some producers are also now making steamed and pan-fried green teas for speciality markets.

Dunsandle FOP Organic

Situated in the lofty mountains of the famous Nilgiri Highlands, the Dunsandle FOP Organic estate overlooks the Indian Ocean.

Character
This bright, fragrant tea is possibly one of the few teas left in South India with all the character, flavour and appearance of a traditionally produced orthodox Nilgiri. The larger leaf contains some tips and brews a light amber-coloured infusion that has a delicate, slightly fruity flavour.

Dunsandle FOP Organic cup

Dunsandle FOP Organic dry

Brewing Tips
Brew 2.5g (0.09oz) in 200ml (7fl oz) water at 100°C (212°F) for 3–4 minutes.

Dunsandle FOP Organic wet

Burnside Frost

Character
The contrasting leaf has a distinctive aroma and flavour profile. Flagrantly fragrant, it is a high-grown black tea with an appetizing greenness to its flavour.

Brewing Tips
Infuse 3.5g (0.12oz) in 200ml (7fl oz) water at 100°C (212°F) for 4–5 minutes.

Burnside Frost dry

Nilgiri Green

Several factories are now making steamed and pan-fired green teas. Coonoor Tea Estate and Parkside Tea Estate are turning clonal leaf grown in organic conditions at an altitude of 1981m (6,500ft) into a range of fascinating and attractive interesting teas. Pluckers gather just one bud and one leaf from the bushes and these are then panned, rolled and dried in machines that were carefully chosen and imported from China.

Hari Khukri Boutique Green

Character
Long, twisted, unbroken leaves give an amber-gold liquor with the aroma and taste of freshly mown grass. This may also be marketed as Blue Mountain Green.

Brewing Tips
Brew 2.5g (0.09oz) in 200ml (7fl oz) water at 75°C (167° F) for 1½–2 minutes

Hari Khukri Boutique cup

Hari Khukri Boutique dry

Hari Khukri Boutique wet

Sikkim

Sikkim is a small tea-growing area on the eastern side of the Himalayan mountains, to the north of Darjeeling and bordering Tibet, Nepal and Bhutan. Its dramatic mountain peaks, lush green valleys and cascading rivers create a breathtaking backdrop for the tea bushes. The only tea plantation is Temi, established in 1969 on an area of approximately 160 hectares (400 acres), and the teas produced here are similar in character to Darjeelings but more full-bodied and fruity.

Temi

Character
The greeny-brown leaves are beautifully twisted with plenty of golden tip and give a powerful, sweet fruity aroma and a deliciously fragrant, almost honey-like flavour.

Brewing Tips
Brew 2.5g (0.09oz) in 200ml (7fl oz) water at 93°C (200°F) for 2 minutes.

Temi cup

Temi dry

Temi wet

Indonesia

Tea cultivation was started by the Dutch East India Company on Sumatra in the early eighteenth century. The first plants were grown from seed imported from China but they did not flourish and were replaced with Assam bushes brought from India. In the early part of the twentieth century, Indonesian teas dominated the European and British markets. However, the World War II brought with it a major decline in the industry, which did not recover until the 1980s when a rehabilitation programme began. Since then, there has been constant improvement, modernization of factories and the replanting of old estates, and the Research Institute for Tea has worked with the industry to increase tea production and improve quality. Approximately 70 per cent of the tea is grown on plantations located in the highlands of the island of Java on volcanic soil, where the tropical climate encourages vigorous growth. Leaves are plucked throughout the year, with the best quality resulting from the late summer harvest in August and September. In the past, all teas were black orthodox but some estates now manufacture CTC teas to meet the growing demand for teabag blends. Green tea production, mostly by smallholder farmers, was introduced in the 1980s and now accounts for approximately 60 per cent of total output. Most of the green tea is consumed locally.

Java Malabar

Character
Deep brown, lightly twisted large pieces of leaf give a rich amber-coloured liquor that has a sweet, very smooth, slightly spicy taste and aroma with raisin undertones.

Brewing Tips
Brew 2.5–3g (0.09–0.10oz) in 200ml (7fl oz) of boiling water for 3–4 minutes.

Java Malabar cup

Java Malabar dry

Java Malabar wet

Japan

In the early days of cultivation in Japan, tea was plucked by hand. Today, however, almost all tea is harvested by machine. The disadvantage of mechanical harvesting is that the machine cannot tell the difference between tender new leaf buds and shoots and older, tougher stems and leaves. The Japanese method of gathering the leaves also gives plantations in Japan a different appearance from those in other parts of the world. The bushes are planted side by side in long rows, creating waves of green across the gently rolling countryside, and as the machines are guided over the top of the bushes, so a curved 'plucking table' develops. (In regions where bushes are picked by hand, the plucking table is much flatter). Whereas in most tea-growing countries a certain amount of manual work is still involved, the Japanese tea industry is mechanized throughout the entire manufacturing process –

from picking and steaming the leaves to rolling, drying, sorting and packing. It is only the most special and expensive of the Gyokuros and Kariganes that are hand plucked and manufactured.

The Japanese growing areas are all in hilly parts of the country close to rivers, streams and lakes where the climate is misty and damp and the amount of hot sunshine is tempered by cooler, hazy mornings and softer light. The harvest begins at the end of April and between two and four crops are gathered each year before the late autumn weather brings a period of dormancy. The majority of teas produced in Japan are green and the varieties vary according to the time of year the leaves are picked, the part of the plant used and the manufacturing method employed. However, one or two producers also make very small quantities of black tea. Black tea was first manufactured in Japan in the 1870s, peaked in the 1950s and then steadily declined. Various cultivars are used, the most recent of which is called *Benihuki*, a hybrid of *Camellia sinensis* grown in Darjeeling and an Assam varietal created at the National Institute of Vegetable and Tea Science in Makurazaki, Kagoshima.

Japanese bushes, grown for Gyokuro, are shaded for about 20 days before hand plucking begins. Here the canvas covers have been rolled back.

Green teas

Gyokuro

Gyokuro is Japan's most expensive, highest quality tea and it is grown, picked and processed with extreme care and skill. The bushes are kept under 90 per cent shade for about 20 days prior to harvesting. Just as the new leaf buds start to form, the bushes are covered with bamboo, reed or canvas mats and the reduced light forces the plant to produce a higher concentration of chlorophyll and darker green leaves.

Character
The neat flat needles are a deep rich green flecked with hints of yellow and paler green. The infusion is clear pale yellow and the aroma and flavour sweet, mild and very smooth.

Brewing Tips
Brew 9g (0.32oz) in 80ml (3fl oz) water at 60°C (140°F) for 2–3 minutes. Strain and drink and add more water for a further infusion.

Gyokuro dry cup

Gyokuro dry

Gyokuro wet

Matcha

Matcha, the very fine green powdered tea used for the Japanese Tea Ceremony, is made by grinding Tencha, a finely chopped tea made in the same way as Gyokuro. Before the leaves are gathered, the bushes are shaded in the same way as for Gyokuro and then slightly larger leaves are harvested, steamed and dried but are not rolled. Instead the veins and stems are removed and the remaining leaf parts are ground to a very fine powder. To prepare this for the Tea Ceremony, the powder is whisked into hot water with a specially crafted bamboo whisk.

Character
The finely ground powder is a vibrant lime green. When whisked into hot water, the tea dissolves, giving a thin, frothy, intensely green drink that has a distinctive grassy flavour.

Brewing Tips
Warm a bowl and a whisk with hot water, then tip the water away. Measure two thirds of a teaspoon of Matcha into the bowl and gently pour in 60ml (2fl oz) water at 80°C (175°F), and whisk briskly to make a foamy liquid.

Matcha dry

Kukicha

Kukicha is made from the stems and stalks that are removed from the leaves used in the production of Sencha (see page 175). The higher the quality of the stalks and stems, the finer the flavour of the tea.

Character
The tea is a mixture of dark green leaves and stalky, fibrous, straw-coloured pieces. The infusion is pale yellow-green and it has a light fragrance and a clean, sweet, almost nutty flavour.

Brewing Tips
Brew 7g (0.25oz) in 240ml (8¼fl oz) water at 90°C (194°F) for 30–60 seconds. Strain and drink and add more water for a second infusion.

Kukicha dry

Karigane

Karigane is made from the stems and stalks that remain after Gyokuro has been manufactured, so, like Gyokuro, the bushes are heavily shaded for approximately a month before the tea is plucked and processed.

Character
The lime-green and dark jade stems and stalks yield an exquisitely delicate and clear, pale green liquor that is milky smooth, subtly grassy and sweet. A sublime tea!

Brewing Tips
Brew 7g (0.25oz) in 240ml (8¼fl oz) of water at 50–55°C (122–131°F) for 1½–2 minutes. Strain and add more water for three further infusions.

Karigane cup

Karigane dry

Karigane wet

Sencha

Sencha is made from the first picking of the leaves in spring. The freshly picked leaves are steamed (in order to de-enzyme the tea and enhance the green colour), followed by alternate drying and rolling. Sencha has a high vitamin C content.

Character
The long, flat, emerald green needles of tea are flecked with hints of pale green and give a light golden-yellow infusion. The delicately sweet aroma and flavour are reminiscent of freshly mown grass and sea breezes.

Brewing Tips
Brew 6g (0.21oz) in 160ml (5.5fl oz) water at 80°C (175°F) for 2 minutes. Strain and drink and add more water for a second infusion.

Sencha cup

Sencha dry

Sencha wet

Bancha

Bancha is made from the summer and autumn picking of the leaves when the stalks and leaves are tougher and coarser than those gathered earlier in the year to make Sencha. Bancha is less fine and delicate in taste but has a high fluoride content and is therefore considered to be beneficial to the health of the teeth.

Character
Bancha has a coarser appearance than Sencha and is more yellow-green in colour. The infusion is a deeper golden-yellow and the aroma and flavour stronger, more astringent and less fragrant.

Brewing Tips
Brew 4.5g (0.16oz) in 200ml (7fl oz) water at 100°C (212°F) for 15–30 seconds.

Bancha wet

Houjicha

Houjicha is made by roasting or pan frying Sencha or Bancha. The idea of roasting green leaves was invented in 1920 by a Kyoto merchant who had a surplus stock of old green leaves which he did not want to waste. The colour of the leaf changes during the firing from green to biscuity-brown and the flavour is less astringent than that of the green tea.

Character
The leaves are toasty brown and have a sweet, biscuity smell. The infusion is rich amber in colour and has a mild, slightly biscuity, caramel aroma and flavour.

Brewing Tips
Brew 4.5g (0.16oz) in 200ml (7 fl oz) water at 100°C (212°F) for 15–30 seconds.

Houjicha cup

Houjicha dry

Houjicha wet

Genmaicha

In English, this means 'rice tea' as hulled rice kernels and popped corn are mixed with Bancha or medium-grade Sencha.

Character
The mixture of tea and grains gives a bright golden liquor that has a nutty, slightly savoury aroma and flavour.

Brewing Tips
Brew 4.5g (0.16oz) in 200ml (7fl oz) water at 100°C (212 F) for 15–30 seconds.

Genmaicha cup

Genmaicha dry

Genmaicha wet

Japanese 'Yumehuki' Black

Character

This unusual tea is made by Kyoko Tanaka, curator of the Anglo-Satsuma Museum in Kyushu and green tea adviser. When the leaf has been plucked (Kyoko usually gets four harvests a year between spring and autumn), it is withered, rolled both by machine and by hand, oxidized in a machine and then dried. The neat, broken leaf gives a beautiful coppery red liquor with a rich aroma – a liquor that is surprisingly punchy with a sweet spiciness and warm tones of sun-warmed wood.

Brewing Tips

Brew 2.5 g (0.09oz) in 200ml (7fl oz) of boiling water for 3 minutes.

Yumehuki cup

Yumehuki dry

Yumehuki wet

Kenya

Because Kenya is situated right on the equator, there are very few fluctuations in the weather and tea grows throughout the year. Bushes were first planted here in 1903 when white settlers experimented with a few tea bushes at Limuru in Kiambu District and production slowly increased in the Kenya Highlands of Kericho and Nandi.

The lower land is too hot for the tea bush to thrive and so the plantations are situated high up at altitudes ranging from 1,300 to 2,200m (4,500 to 7,000ft) where the volcanic soil provides excellent growing conditions, where the air is cooler and where moist air rises from Lake Victoria and falls as rain over the mountains. Today, the plantations cover 400 square miles and are home to more than a billion bushes. Plucking is almost entirely carried out by hand and, on average, each plucker gathers approximately 30,000 new leaf shoots every day. Although the Kenyan bushes flush all year, the very best crops are harvested from late January to early February.

In 1950 the Tea Board of Kenya was established in order to oversee what was becoming an important cash crop for the country. In 1965, the Kenya Tea Development Authority (KTDA) was founded with the objective of promoting and supporting the cultivation of tea by smallholder farmers in suitable areas of the country. Today more than 12 per cent of the population work in the tea industry and about half a million people are actually involved in tea production. The KTDA now has 430,000 smallholder farmers growing and selling tea to a total of 98 tea factories – 55 factories under KTDA management and others owned by multinational tea companies. The total processing capacity of the KTDA factories is approximately 75,000 tonnes (73,815 tons) of green leaf per annum.

Most companies manufacture CTC teas for teabag blends but, with a growing interest around the world in speciality orthodox teas, the KTDA has recently diversified into orthodox manufacture at Kangaita Tea Estate. Clonal tea plants were carefully selected to produce an excellent selection of large-leafed teas, orthodox machinery was imported from India and the teas are so successful that there is now talk of extending the orthodox manufacture.

Some Kenyan producers are now also making different styles of white and green 'natural' teas. These are grown at high altitudes where pesticides are not necessary and where the tight weave of the plucking table means that no weeds can grow and therefore no herbicides are needed. The teas are strictly seasonal in order to achieve the best possible quality and character and involve minimal handling so the leaf often looks rather mixed and somewhat different from other, more conventional teas. The white teas are naturally dried as far as possible and a final mechanical drying is used to drive off any excess moisture. The unoxidized greens are neither steamed nor pan fired but simply twisted in a rotorvane and then dried.

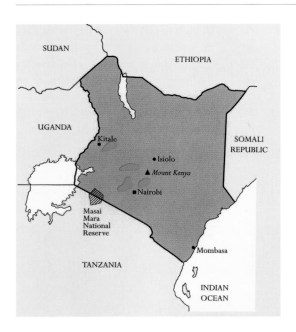

Kenya BOP Blend

Small-leafed Kenya teas are often used to give strength and colour to breakfast blends but they also drink well alone. They are especially good with rich chocolate foods.

Character
Dark brown small leaf that gives a rich red liquor and has a good, strong, balanced flavour.

Brewing Tips
Infuse 2.5g (0.09oz) in 200ml (7fl oz) water at 100°C (212°F) for 2–3 minutes.

Kenya BOP Blend cup

Kangaita OP

Grown on plantations owned by the
Kenya Tea Development Agency,
these high-quality black teas are now
reaching a niche speciality market
around the world.

Character
Neat browny-black leaf that gives a
warm dark amber infusion and has a
satisfying, warm aroma and a smooth
but powerful flavour.

Brewing Tips
Infuse 2.5g (0.09oz) in 200ml
(7fl oz) water at 100°C (212°F) for
4–5 minutes.

Kangaita OP cup

Kangaita OP dry

Kangaita OP wet

Kenya Silverback White

Character
One of the 'natural' range, these shiny, silver-green buds, mixed with tiny flakes that have broken off during handling, brew to give a pale amber liquor that has a slightly green aroma with a hint of toast, and a smooth, peachy sweet taste with undertones of toasted barley.

Brewing Tips
Brew 2.5g (0.09oz) in 200ml (7fl oz) water at 75°C (167°F) for 3 minutes.

Kenya Silverback White cup

Kenya Silverback White dry

Kenya Silverback White wet

Kenya Safari Nandi White

Character
Another 'natural' tea, silvery buds mixed with sage greeny-yellow whole and broken leaf give a golden liquor that is smooth and gentle and has the aroma of old-fashioned roses and warm hay.

Brewing Tips
Brew 2.5g (0.09oz) in 200ml (7fl oz) water at 75°C (167°F) for 3 minutes.

Kenya Safari Nandi White cup

Kenya Safari Nandi White dry

Kenya Safari Nandi White wet

Kenya 'Natural' Green Tea

Character
Plucked from bushes that grow at high altitudes, the leaf is simply broken in a rotorvane and dried. It is unsorted and so shows a mixture of grades including flake, fibre and small dust particles. The dry leaf brews to give a light copper liquor that has a distinctly floral aroma and a smooth, cut grass character with tantalising hints of summer roses.

Brewing Tips
Brew 2.5g (0.09oz) in 200ml (7fl oz) water at 80°C (175°F) for 3 minutes

Kenya Natural Green Tea cup

Kenya Natural Green Tea dry

Kenya Natural Green Tea wet

South Korea

It is thought that tea was introduced into Korea in the second or third century AD by Buddhist monks returning from China and, as well as being the luxury drink of the privileged classes, it also played an important part in Buddhist ceremonies and traditions. Tea was sent as a gift to respected monks who both offered it to the Buddha and drank it themselves as a way of disciplining the mind and of creating an atmosphere of communion and harmony. When Confucianism replaced Buddhism in the fourteenth century, Buddhist temples were destroyed, tea drinking was repressed and many monks fled to the

mountains where they lived almost as hermits and developed their own tea tradition. In a few places, tea plants that had been established earlier continued to grow as wild bushes and local people drank an infusion from the plucked and dried leaves. Today, those same bushes are still being plucked to make very special green teas.

Tea drinking traditions among the ordinary people were further disrupted by the Japanese invasions of the 1590s and rice wine became the accepted drink that was served and offered during ritualistic ceremonies and events. However, remnants of the tea tradition survived as a ritual part

Very young spring-picked leaves and buds ready for manufacture.

of Korean culture rather than as an everyday drink. Then, in the early nineteenth century, a revival of interest started when the Confucian scholar Chong Yag-yong was exiled to the south of the country and learned the method of making and drinking tea from the monks there. He passed his interest on to a young Buddhist monk, Cho ui, who established a special hermitage in the hills above Taehung-sa and wrote a now-famous poem in praise of tea. This led eventually to a new movement in the 1970s, inspired by the Venerable Hyo Dang who organised the rebuilding of the dilapidated hermitage and wrote *The Way of Tea*, the first book on

tea to be published in modern Korea. In 1945, he also founded schools and universities of tea and this has resulted in a very strong tea culture in the country today.

South Korea's plantations are all in the southern part of the country to the south of Chonju. Small areas of bushes grow on the slopes of Chiri-san; larger, industrial-scale estates are in Bosong near Kangjin and on the slopes of Wolch'ul-san in the south-west. The rows of bushes look rather like those grown in Japan in that the plucking table is smoothly rounded rather than flat. The plants begin to sprout in early April and the finest teas are made from leaves and buds

In Korea, the leaf is de-enzymed and dried in a large wok.

that are hand-picked (mainly by the women) during the first two months of the growing season. After May, the leaves are coarser and no longer give the intense flavour and fragrance required in the best teas.

The most expensive and finest teas, called U-jeon, are made before the first Spring festival of Kok-u which falls round about 20 April. Teas made between Kok-u and Ipha, the next festival on 5 or 6 May are called Se-jark. Teas made after Ipha are called Jung-jark. Teas made after May 15th are called Dae-jark. If weather patterns vary from the norm and the spring frosts and cold temperatures linger, the manufacturing dates may continue beyond the traditional festivals. The earlier in the season the teas are made, the more delicate the aroma and flavour and the cooler the water used for brewing should be. Most of the growing quantity of teas made every year are green (known as Nokcha) and are divided into two types – Puch'o-ch'a (the most commonly made type) and Chung-ch'a (less common).

To make Puch'o-ch'a, the leaves must be dried to de-enzyme them within 24 hours of plucking and in an industrial situation, this is done inside a revolving drum which blows warm air over the tea. In artisinal situations, the leaves are hand-dried by tossing them in a hot iron pan set over a wood or gas fire. The softened leaves are then rolled or rubbed to shape them and Korean green tea often has a lightly curled or twisted appearance. After the initial rolling, the leaf is returned to the pan and dried again and these two stages are repeated up to nine times until the leaf is almost completely dry.

To make Chung-ch'a, freshly plucked leaves are plunged into near-boiling water, drained, dried in a hot pan where the shaping and drying go on simultaneously. The workers wear gloves to protect their hands from the hot metal as they press, twist and turn the leaf until it is almost totally dry. It is a skilful job as the leaf must not burn and so must be constantly turned and moved around in the bottom of the large wok-like pan. A third, less common green variety is Jengjae-cha, which is made by steaming the leaf for 30–40 seconds and then drying it. The leaf retains its fresh green colour and gives a liquor with a character similar to Japanese Senchas.

The Korean tea ceremony.

Nokcha

Character
Nokcha means simply 'green tea' and
this rare example comes from a
mountain in Bosong with the
wonderful name of 'In the Middle of
a Dream'. The beautifully curled leaf
gives a clear amber liquor with a
deliciously sweet and biscuity aroma
and taste.

Brewing Tips
Brew 2.5g (0.09oz) in 200ml
(7fl oz) water at 60–70°C
(140–158°F) for up to 1¼ minutes.
Strain and add more water for a
further three infusions.

Nokcha cup

Nokcha dry

Nokcha wet

Sparrow's Tongue
(Chaksol Cha)

Character

This is Korea's most famous green tea
and is sometimes called 'Woojeon'. It
is made from the very smallest spring
buds that are usually picked between
20th April and the beginning of May
and the name reflects the size and
pointy shape of the lightly twisted,
olive green leaves. The freshly
plucked leaves are repeatedly roasted,
rubbed and roasted again over a
charcoal fire. This particular tea is
harvested during the first week of
May from bushes growing in Hwagae,
near the famous mountain Chiri-san,
and the tiny buds yield a liquor that is
clear pale amber-green and has a
wonderful sweet aroma and a smooth,
elegant, slightly dry, vegetal quality.

Brewing Tips

Brew 2.5g (0.09 oz) in 200 ml (7 fl oz)
of water at 50–55° C (122–131°F) for
up to 1½ minutes. Strain and add
more water for three infusions.

Sparrow's Tongue cup

Sparrow's Tongue dry

Sparrow's Tongue wet

Korean Black

Although most of the South
Korean teas are green, some
people also hand-make small
quantities of black tea.

Character
Large, peaty-black, twisted
whole leaves have a taut wiry
appearance with occasional
flecks of furry tip. The liquor
is a beautiful coppery amber
and the taste is slightly woody
with hints of raisins and a
sweet, lingering aftertaste.

Brewing Tips
Brew 2.5g (0.09oz) in 200 ml
(7 fl oz) water at 100°C (212°F)
for 4 minutes.

Korean Black cup

Korean Black dry

Korean Black wet

Malawi

Tea cultivation started in Malawi in 1878 when tea seeds were taken from the Royal Botanic Gardens in Edinburgh and planted on land in what was then called Nyasaland. When plantations were established in the lowlands of Mulanje and Thyolo in the Shire Highlands, the seeds used came from Natal in South Africa where plants had originally been transplanted from Ceylon. Unpredictable weather patterns can make tea-growing difficult for the Malawi planters but the introduction of more clonal plants has helped ease this problem. Malawi was in fact the first African country to introduce clonal methods of estate refurbishment.

The main picking season is during Malawi's summer from October to April, when plenty of rain encourages the bushes to flush continuously. Today, Malawi exports more than 35,000 tonnes (34,447 tons) every year and, after Kenya, is Africa's second most important tea-producing country. In the past, all the teas were CTC blacks, valued for their wonderful bright colour and rich flavour that adds quality to both teabag and loose-leaf blends but today, as in other African tea regions, producers here are manufacturing more unusual speciality teas. For example, Satemwa Tea Estates Ltd, a third-generation company founded in the 1920s in the Shire Highlands just north of Blantyre, are co-ordinating and marketing hand-made white and green teas produced by smallholder farmers. Nigel Melican of Teacraft Ltd (UK consultant to the international tea industry) started working with Satamwa to develop these teas in 2006. Until then, no one realized that leaf plucked from the African assamica-type bushes (traditionally turned into strong, red-liquoring, CTC black teas) could be used to make delicate white teas that have a floral scent a little like wild rose petals, and gentle greens that have a fruity apricot note. The combined output of hand-made teas made by the smallholder farmers and Satemwa is about two tonnes (1.9 tons) a year.

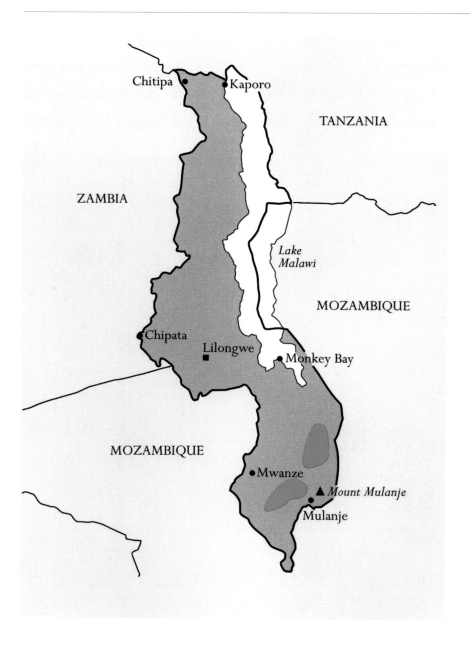

Chitipa

Kaporo

TANZANIA

ZAMBIA

Lake
Malawi

MOZAMBIQUE

Chipata

Lilongwe

Monkey Bay

MOZAMBIQUE

Mwanze

Mount Mulanje

Mulanje

Namingomba Black

Character
Good-quality, pure clonal, small-leafed CTC tea that gives a coppery red infusion and a full-bodied flavour. Drinks well with milk.

Brewing Tips
Infuse 2.5g (0.09 oz) in 200ml (7fl oz) water at 100°C (212°F) for 3 minutes.

Namingomba Black cup

Namingomba Black dry

Namingomba Black wet

Salima Peony

Character
Made from new shoots of two leaves and a bud gathered from the Salima tea bush varietal, the dark, chocolate brown leaves are mixed with silvery buds and stems. The liquor is clear pale gold and has a sweet, flowery aroma and a light, fruity taste with lingering notes of green apple.

Brewing Tips
Brew 2.5g (0.09oz) in 200ml (7fl oz) water at 75°C (167°F) for up to 5 minutes. Strain and add more water for several more infusions.

Salima Peony cup

Salima Peony dry

Salima Peony wet

Mulanje Needles

Character
This is made from the fine, wiry buds of the Mulanje varietal and gives a pale, orangey-golden liquor with sweet floral tones and hints of ripe red apples. Similar 'needle' teas are also made from other local varietals (Zomba and Chilwa) and have the same elegant striped silvery appearance.

Brewing Tips
Brew 2.5g (0.09oz) in 200ml (7fl oz) water at 75°C (167°F) for up to 5 minutes. Strain and add more water for several further infusions.

Mulanje Needles cup

Mulanje Needles dry

Mulanje Needles wet

Antlers d'Amour

Character
An exceptional tea and unique even
among Malawi hand-made teas, the
Antlers are made from just the juicy
stems at the very tip of each shoot
where the delicate aroma is most
concentrated and great skill and care
is needed to make this very rare and
special tea. The leaves and leaf buds
are carefully nipped off for
manufacture as 'needle' and 'peony'
types and the name 'antlers' comes
from the fact that the dry stems that
are left are velvety and have the
appearance of deers' antlers in the
early spring. They yield a light amber-
coloured liquor that has the aroma of
gentle rose petal sweetness and the
taste and soft undertones of sun-
warmed wood.

Brewing Tips
Brew 2.5–3g (0.09–0.10oz) in 200ml
(7fl oz) water at 75°C (167°F) for up
to 5 minutes. Strain and add more
water for several further infusions.

Antlers d'Amour cup

Antlers d'Amour dry

Antlers d'Amour wet

Malaysia

The first tea plantation in Malaysia was established in the Cameron Highlands in 1929 by the son of a British civil servant who named it Boh after Bohea, the mountainous district of China's Fujian province where black tea was made and exported to Europe. Named after William Cameron, the Scottish surveyor who discovered the area in 1885, the region is known as 'Malaysia's Green Bowl' and enjoys a combination of all the best features for tea production – moderate temperatures, plenty of rain and sunshine, good soil that drains well and high altitudes. Boh Plantations Sdn Bhd now owns four gardens – Boh, Sungei Palas, Fairlie in the Cameron Highlands and Bukit Cheeding in Selangor – and produces roughly 4,000 tonnes (3,937 tons) of tea every year. This is roughly 70 per cent of Malaysia's tea in what are almost perfect conditions for the tea plant. Other tea plantations in the area are the Bharat Tea Estate and Blue Valley Plantation. The orthodox teas that are produced here give a light, bright smooth liquor and a rich golden colour.

For those who would like to enjoy more than the excellent teas produced in this region, Cameron Highlands Resort has now added a 56-room spa resort that offers guests visits to the tea plantations, ancient tea rituals, tea baths, tea tastings, tea plantation picnics and elegant afternoon teas.

Boh Palas Supreme

Character
A Flowery Pekoe, neatly twisted, orthodox black tea gives a bright, coppery liquor that has a raisin-sweet aroma and a light, smooth taste.

Brewing Tips
Brew 2.5–3g (0.09–0.10oz) in 200ml (7fl oz) boiling water for 4 minutes.

Boh Palas Supreme cup

Boh Palas Supreme dry

Boh Palas Supreme wet

Nepal

While on a tour of Darjeeling in 1873, Colonel Gajraj Singh Thapa tasted the tea there and was so impressed that he determined to cultivate the plant in Nepal, where he was Governor-general. He established two plantations at Ilam and Soktim where the first Nepalese orthodox teas were produced. In 1985, five eastern regions of the country – Jhapa, Ilam, Panchthar, Terhathum and Dhankuta – were declared a 'tea-zone' by the government and since then three new plantations and seven new factories have been established. Since 1920, the land area under tea has increased from 94 hectares (233 acres) to 810 hectares (2,000 acres), and production has increased from 2 tonnes (1.9 tons) to 1,000 tonnes (984.2 tons). The gardens are situated at altitudes ranging from 915 metres (3,000 feet) to 1,830 metres (6,000 feet) above sea level and the plants grown are mostly of the China variety, as this more easily withstands the mountains' cold temperatures. The teas, which are all black, are grown on approximately 5,000 family smallholdings and 100 or so larger gardens and estates, and processed in 16 CTC and 11 orthodox factories. After a period of dormancy in the icy winter months, the first new shoots begin to appear in late February and are gathered through to April to make the First Flush, which gives a pale golden-coloured liquor and a soft, delicate flavour. In May and June, the Second Flush is gathered to give a slightly more mature tea that has a fuller taste and a fruity character. From mid-June to the end of September, the region is drenched by the monsoon rains and the teas made during this season have a higher water content, a darker colour and stronger flavour. October's autumn teas have a much richer aroma and a marked muscatel flavour.

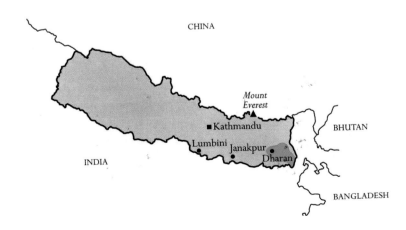

First Flush Guranse Organic

Character
The leaves of this exquisite tea are blackish-brown with lots of tip. The tea brews to an amber cup and has a woody aroma and a clean, refreshing, sweet floral flavour, similar to Darjeeling.

Brewing Tips
Brew 2.5g (0.09oz) in 200ml (7fl oz) water at 100°C (212°F) for 3–4 minutes.

First Flush Guranse Organic dry

Nepal Autumnal

Character
The leaves are a mixture of silver, green and brown with a scattering of golden tips. The infusion is a clear pale honey colour and has a soft, slightly nutty aroma and flavour.

Brewing Tips
Brew 2.5g (0.09oz) in 200ml (7fl oz) water at 100°C (212°F) for 3–4 minutes.

Nepal Autumnal cup

Nepal Autumnal dry

Nepal Autumnal wet

Rwanda

The Rwandan tea industry was established in the 1950s and, with fertile soil and plentiful rainfall, tea flourished here. The civil war of the 1990s led to the complete demise of the industry and it took a while to get the industry back on track but today, excellent quality teas are being made and total production has gone up from 12,700 tonnes (12,500 tons) in 2003 to nearly 17,273 tonnes (17,000 tons) in 2006. Figures for 2007 were expected to be even better. The teas are mostly CTC black but some greens are manufactured and the production of some orthodox blacks is planned for the near future. The tea industry is currently being privatized and the last few publicly owned factories will soon also be in private hands. A new Tea Board will be responsible for the development of the tea sector and will work to co-ordinate the work of the smallholder growers and the processing factories. Some factories are expected to grow their own tea as well as also purchasing plucked leaf from the smallholder farmers.

Thick waterproof aprons protect the pluckers from the harsh trunks and stems of the bushes. Umbrellas provide shade from the intense sun.

Gisovu

Character
Small CTC black, grainy leaf
brews to give a rich, coppery
liquor that is punchy, strong
and packed with flavour.

Brewing Tips
Brew 2.5g (0.09oz) in 200ml
(7fl oz) of boiling water for
2–3 minutes.

Gisovu cup

Gisovu dry

Gisovu wet

Sri Lanka

Until the 1860s, the main crop grown on the teardrop-shaped island of Ceylon was coffee, but when the coffee-rust fungus brought devastation to the estates in 1869, planters were forced to diversify if they were to avoid total ruin. At Loolecondera Estate, tea had been considered as an alternative as early as the 1850s and in 1866 the owners chose James Taylor, a tough, determined and extremely hard-working Scot, to oversee the first sowings of tea seeds on the plantation. With some basic knowledge that he had acquired in India, Taylor started manufacturing black tea on the veranda of his bungalow, rolling the leaf by hand and drying the oxidized leaf in clay stoves heated over charcoal fires. After the success of the first teas, a fully equipped factory was set up in 1872 and the first Ceylon teas were shipped to England and sold at the London auctions in 1873. From those experimental beginnings, the Ceylon tea industry grew rapidly, with production increasing from 10.45kg (23lb) of tea in 1880 to nearly 23 tonnes (22.6 tons) in 1890. In 1883, the first Ceylon tea auction was held in the capital Colombo by a company called Mssrs. Sommerville & Co. The auctions today handle almost 6,000 tonnes (5,905 tons) of tea every week, making Colombo the world's largest auction centre. Exports from the island have increased from 215,000 tonnes (211,604 tons) in 1990 to 288,000 tonnes (283,451 tons) in 2000, a growth of 34 per cent.

In 1993, with a growing demand worldwide for small-leafed teas suitable for the teabag market, the government encouraged producers (by offering financial incentives) to convert from orthodox to CTC manufacturing, but the experiment was not a success and 40 or so factories have now returned to orthodox production. The CTC factories that operate today are mostly in the low-grown areas and are enjoying increasing support from international buyers who seek good-quality teas for teabag manufacture. Some producers have now entered the 'value added' market by packing

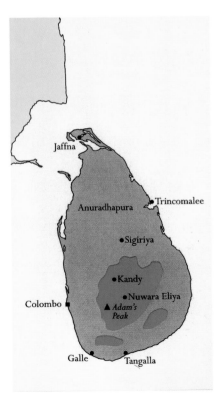

flavoured teas, loose teas and teabags at the factory rather than exporting their teas in bulk, and others have started producing green and organic teas to meet a changing world market. After a decade of problems and uncertainty, the industry has gained a new level of stability, with increasing orders from important markets in the former Soviet Union, the UAE, Syria, Turkey, Iran, Saudi Arabia, Iraq, Egypt, Japan and the UK.

Sri Lanka's plantations are situated at elevations of between 460 and 2,450m (1,500 and 8,000ft) in the central southern part of the island. There are six main growing areas – Ratnapura, a low to mid-growing area about 88km (55 miles) east of the capital Colombo; Galle, a low-growing region situated in the south of the country; Kandy, the mid-growing area around the ancient capital, where the first plantations were established; Dimbula, a high-growing region west of the central mountains; Uva, also a high-growing area that lies to the west of Dimbula; and Nuwara Eliya, the highest tea region, which produces some of the very finest of Ceylon teas.

Each area has its own weather patterns and geographic features and it is these that give the individual teas their characteristic flavours and aromas. Low-grown teas are of good quality but sometimes lack the brisk, bright flavour of the higher-grown teas and so are more often used in blending. The mid-grown teas have greater richness and strength and give good colour, while the high-grown teas are considered to be the best of Sri Lanka's production, giving a beautiful golden infusion and a powerful intensity of flavour. In Dimbula, the best teas are made in the dry season from December to March. The teas give a typically smooth, bright liquor, a delicate perfume and a rich golden flavour. In Uva, a desiccating wind blows through the bushes in late July and August causing the bushes to almost close up on themselves in self-protection. So, once the wind has passed, the peak quality teas made in September have a concentration of flavour unlike any other tea form anywhere else in the world.

Dimbula

Kirkoswold

The important growing area of Dimbula covers the western slopes of the island's tea-growing region. The monsoon brings torrential rain during August and September and the best teas are gathered from December to March/April. The teas produced here are noted for their body and strength and wonderful aroma and vary through the season from full bodied to lighter and more fragrant.

Character
The leaves from this award-winning estate yield a coppery-coloured cup with golden notes and a full-bodied flavour.

Brewing Tips
Brew 2.5g (0.09oz) in 200ml (7fl oz) water at 100°C (212°F) for 4 minutes.

Kirkoswold cup

Kirkoswold dry

Kirkoswold wet

Galle

Lumbini Estate

The teas from the low-growing region of Galle in the south of the island are noted for their large, very black leaf, stylish appearance and the high level of golden and silvery tips. The success of the teas has led to an increase in the number of small private planters growing tea here.

Character
This tea gives a very rich, strong and smooth infusion that has the smoky overtones of a China black. It drinks well with milk.

Brewing Tips
Brew 2.5g (0.09oz) in 200ml (7fl oz) water at 100°C (212°F) for 4 minutes.

Lumbini Estate cup

Lumbini Estate dry

Lumbini Estate wet

Nuwara Eliya

Lovers' Leap

The tea from Nuwara Eliya, Sri Lanka's highest tea-growing region, is often referred to as Sri Lanka's 'champagne of teas' and is sought after by tea-drinkers all over the world. The best teas of the area give a beautiful, golden liquor that is light, smooth and bright, and has an exquisite perfume.

Character
The brisk caramel liquor has a flowery aroma and a light flavour that is wonderful to drink after dinner.

Brewing Tips
Brew 2.5g (0.09oz) in 200ml (7fl oz) water at 100°C (212°F) for 4–5 minutes.

Lovers' Leap cup

Lovers' Leap dry

Lovers' Leap wet

Ratnapura

New Vithanakande

The tea gardens in the south-western, low-growing Ratnapura region are protected from the drying winds of the south-western monsoon by the forest belt of the Sinharaja Forest Reserve that lies just to the south. The teas produced here are full bodied, thick and strong.

Character
The beautifully tippy, wiry leaves produce a bright amber cup that has a distinctive aroma and a smooth caramel finish.

Brewing Tips
Infuse 2.5g (0.09oz) in 200ml (7fl oz) water at 100°C (212°F) for 4–5 minutes.

New Vithanakande cup

New Vithanakande dry

New Vithanakande wet

Uva

Uva St James's Estate BOP

The teas from the high eastern slopes of the central mountains in the Uva district have a unique flavour and pungency, caused mainly by the 'Cachan' wind that blows in from the north east at the end of July until mid-August. The teas have an almost medicinal, wintergreen character.

Brewing Tips
Brew 2.5g (0.09oz) in 200ml (7fl oz) water at 100°C (212°F) for 4 minutes.

Character
The copper-coloured infusion has a smooth, pronounced taste and a wonderful aroma. It drinks well with milk.

Uva St James's Estate BOP dry

Uva OP

Character
The neat dark brown leaf is mingled with a few golden flecks of tip. The clear infusion is a beautiful dark amber colour and has an aroma that is reminiscent of warm woodland. The flavour is sweet and mild and intensely satisfying.

Brewing Tips
Brew 2.5g (0.09oz) in 200ml (7fl oz) water at 100°C (212°F) for 3–4 minutes.

Uva OP cup

Uva OP dry

Uva OP wet

Ceylon Silver Needles

Character
Down-covered buds yield a
light flowery liquor that has a
sweet finish.

Brewing Tips
Brew 2.5g (0.09oz) in 200ml
(7fl oz) water at 82°C (180°F)
for 4–7 minutes. Strain and
add more water for three
further infusions.

Ceylon Silver Needles cup

Ceylon Silver Needles dry

Ceylon Silver Needles wet

Taiwan

The cultivation of tea bushes in Formosa (as Taiwan was formerly named) began some two hundred years ago when Chinese migrants from the mainland province of Fujian settled here and brought with them their tea-making skills. The soil, climate and hilly landscape were found to be perfect for the tea plant and in 1869 Englishman John Dodd was responsible for exporting the first Taiwan-made tea from the island when he hired two clippers to sail the teas to New York. By the 1880s, Formosa was famous for its teas and was annually exporting more than 4.5 million kg (10 million lb).

In the 1920s, bushes from Assam were planted in the Sun Moon Lake district of Nantou province by the Japanese who then ruled the island and the leaf was used to make black tea. By the 1960s, this had become an important export for the island but, as Taiwan modernised, the rising cost of production made it difficult to compete with other, cheaper tea-producing countries and most of the plantations were converted to oolong and pouchong manufacture – teas that Taiwan is famous for today. A small amount of black tea is still made but the majority of Taiwan's teas are green unoxidised teas, partially oxidised oolongs (some of which are roasted) and very lightly oxidised pouchongs.

Although early cultivation was concentrated mainly around Taipei, most of the central region of the island is today home to 21,223 hectares (52,468 acres) of

plantations, all above 305 metres (1,000 feet). The teas are grown on family-owned 'boutique tea farms' where the owner/tea master oversees the entire process and passes his or her skills and secret methods of manufacture on to the next generation so that the production of prized teas can continue. Although methods of cultivation and hand-plucking have not changed greatly, the simple tools of the early 20th century have been replaced by modern machinery – such as electric clippers imported from Japan – and some of the farmers have stopped using fertilisers and pesticides in favour of a more organic approach that produces better teas. Taiwan now produces approximately 20,321 tonnes (20,000 tons) of tea every year, exports 2,032 tonnes (2,000 tons) and imports roughly 21,337 tonnes (21,000 tons).

The bush flushes five times between April and December and the finest quality teas are made from leaf gathered from April to the middle of August. It is crucial that the leaves are plucked at the right time – if they are too young, their aroma and flavour will not have fully developed; if they are too mature, the stems will be too coarse. The best teas are made from leaves that are harvested between 10 o'clock in the morning and 2 o'clock in the afternoon when the morning dew has evaporated from the surface of the leaves but when the sun is still strong enough for withering. After withering, the leaves are shaken, pan-fried, rolled and dried.

The methods used and the varieties of tea made vary according to the season and to the location on the island. April is the season for making green, pouchong, some of the fragrant oolongs and small quantities of Lung Ching (Dragon Well) and Pi Lo Chun (also written Bi Luo Chun or Bi Lu Chun and meaning Green Snail Spring), while the White Tip Oolongs (also called Oriental Beauty) are made later in June and July. In Wenshan district to the south east of Taipei city,

In the cloudy damp conditions of the high mountain regions, the Taiwanese pluckers need waterproof clothing.

Pouchong (also written as Baozhong or Paochong), teas are famous for their lightly oxidised, long, open, twisted leaves and floral, bright liquor. Shimen Township to the north of Taipei manufacture slow-smoked Tie Kuan Yin type oolongs and Sansia to the south west of Taipei is famous for its Lung Ching (Dragon Well) green teas. From the rolling hills and mountains of Nantou County come several different oolongs including Tung Ting with its rolled green leaf and characteristic flowery aroma and taste, and Yu Shan (Jade Mountain) which is made from thick leaves and gives a mouth-filling liquor with a wonderful sweet aroma and taste. In the centre of the Nantou county at Sun Moon Lake, black tea is made as the local speciality and lightly oxidised rolled oolongs are also famous. Li Shan (Pear Mountain), in one of Taiwan's highest mountain ranges in the northern half of the island, has plantations at between 1,800 and 2,650 metres (5,900 and 8,695 feet) and produces oolongs that are well known for their thick leaves and sublime fragrant and sweet character, while further south, Alishan, another high-growing region with plantations at altitudes between 1,000 and 2,300 metres (3,280 and 7,545 feet), produces oolongs with a wonderful sweet fragrance and overtones of flowers and fruit.

Although small quantities of green, black and smoky Lapsang Souchong teas are made on the island, approximately 99 per cent of Taiwan's production is of pouchongs and oolongs.

Green teas

Formosa Gunpowder

Character
Taiwanese gunpowders typically give a
strong dark green infusion and have a
memorable, slightly grassy flavour.

Brewing Tips
Brew 2.5g (0.09oz) in 200ml (7fl oz)
water at 87°C (190°F) for 3–4
minutes. Strain and add more water
for a second and third infusion.

Formosa Gunpowder dry

Pouchong teas

Bao Zhong (Jade Pouchong)

Character
Not truly greens, yet not wholly
oolongs, pouchongs are very lightly
(12–18 per cent) oxidised (greener
oolongs undergo 30 per cent
oxidation, dark leafed oolongs 70 per
cent). The leaf is withered in the sun
or indoors, pan-fried, dried twice and
then sorted. This typically open,
slightly twisted, olive green leaf yields
an amber-green liquor that has a
delicate, sweet aroma and a slightly
sweet, delicate, smooth flavour.

Brewing Tips
For the best results, brew 2.5–3g
(0.09–0.10oz) in 200ml (7fl oz) water
at 85°C (185°F) to give multiple
short infusions.

Bao Zhong cup

Bao Zhong dry

Bao Zhong wet

Oolong teas

Ali Shan Oolong

Character
One of Taiwan's finest teas grown on the high altitude, misty slopes of Alishan mountain in Chiayi County, the beautiful, twisted, dense pellets of tea give a pale, clear, greeny-yellow liquor that has an intense, sweet, very slightly toasted aroma and a full, creamy, slightly sappy flavour with distinct green tea notes.

Brewing Tips
Brew 3–4g (0.10–0.14oz) in 200ml (7fl oz) of near boiling water for 1–2 minutes. Strain and add more water for 4–5 further infusions.

Ali Shan Oolong cup

Ali Shan Oolong dry

Ali Shan Oolong wet

Amber Oolong

Character
From Nantou County, this is a medium-oxidized, balled oolong that is dried over charcoal and has curled brown leaf. The dry tea has a fascinating, almost chocolatey aroma and unfurls during brewing to give a liquor that is the treacly colour of amber and has an amazing sweet, fruity, biscuity aroma. The taste is mouth-filling, slightly smoky and reminds the taste buds of dark chocolate.

Brewing Tips
Brew 2.5–3g (0.09–0.10oz) in 200ml (7 fl oz) water at 90°C (194°F) for 1–2 minutes. Strain and add more water for four more infusions.

Amber Oolong cup

Amber Oolong dry

Amber Oolong wet

Dong Fang Mei Ren (also known as Oriental Beauty, White Monkey Oolong, Bai Hao or White Tip Oolong)

Character
Originally devised to compete with popular Darjeeling teas, this tea is only picked once a year, at the end of summer. Its special character depends on jassids (common leafhoppers) who bite the leaf. The liquor has the appearance and strength of a black tea but the complex fragrance of an oolong.

Brewing Tips
Brew 2.5–3g (0.09–0.10oz) in 200ml (7fl oz) water at 85°C (185°F) to give multiple short infusions.

Dong Fang Mei Ren cup

Dong Fang Mei Ren dry

Dong Fang Mei Ren, showing the common leafhopper.

Dong Fang Mei Ren wet

Tung Ting

One of Taiwan's finest oolongs, Tung Ting (the name means 'cold summit') is made with young leaves gathered on the highest plantations above Sungpoling (Pine Bluff). The bushes grow on a hilly plateau that is sheltered by groves of areca palm and giant bamboo.

Character
The young leaves and buds brew a pale greeny-golden cup that has a superb flavour and a subtle floral aroma. It is one of the finest green oolongs.

Brewing Tips
Brew 3g (0.10oz) in 200ml (7fl oz) water at 85°C (185°F) for 1–2 minutes. Strain and add more water for several more short steepings.

Tung Ting cup

Tung Ting dry

Tung Ting wet

Yu Oolong (Jade Oolong)

This is a lightly fermented oolong from Yu Shan (Jade Mountain).

Character
The rich, green, loosely rolled leaves yield a tawny infusion that has a complex, delicate, floral aroma and flavour and a deliciously smooth finish.

Brewing Tips
Brew 3g (0.10oz) in 200ml (7fl oz) water at 85°C (185°F) for 1–2 minutes. Strain and add more water for several further short infusions.

Yu Oolong cup

Yu Oolong dry

Yu Oolong wet

Thailand

In 1949, when Mao Tse-tung established a communist state in China, members of Chiang Kai-shek's defeated Chinese Nationalist Kuomintang Army fled into Burma (Myanmar). When civil war erupted there in the 1960s, the Chinese settlers moved into Chiang Rai province in northern Thailand and made it their home, bringing with them their tea-making skills. Clonal tea bushes were acquired from Taiwan and the leaf harvested to manufacture Taiwanese-style oolong and green teas. In the 1970s, opium cultivation was replaced by tea plantations and in the 1980s, tea experts from Taiwan's Tea Agricultural Research Centre were invited to advise and assist in upgrading tea production. The best gardens are located at altitudes of 1,000–1,400m (3,280–4,593ft) where warm days, cool nights and the damp, misty air create perfect conditions for the bushes. Production is small and the oolong, ginseng oolong, green, jasmine and black teas are mostly consumed within Thailand.

Thai Black

Character
Large, ungraded, bold leaf brews to give an earthy aroma and a rich, mouth-filling liquor that has deep layers of flavour with interesting hints of puerh and chocolate.

Thai Black cup

Brewing Tips
Brew 2.5g (0.09oz) in 200ml (7fl oz) of boiling water for 3–4 minutes.

Thai Black dry

Thai Black wet

Thai Green

Character
The interesting open leaf contains lots of stem and is tinged with a range of colours from olive green to plummy-black. It brews to give an amber green liquor that has a spinach-like aroma and a slightly earthy, astringent taste.

Brewing Tips
Brew 2.5-3g (0.09-0.10oz) in 200ml (7 fl oz) of water at 75° C (167° F) for 2–3 minutes.

Thai Green cup

Thai Green dry

Thai Green wet

Chin Shin Oolong

Character
This memorable, balled, lightly oxidised oolong yields a grassy, green aroma and a sweet, honey-like liquor that has a medium mouthfeel and a long finish.

Brewing Tips
Brew 2.5-3g (0.09-0.10oz) in 200ml water at 75° C (167° F) for 1 minute. Strain and add more water for 3–4 further infusions.

Chin Shin Oolong cup

Chin Shin Oolong dry

Chin Shin Oolong wet

United Kingdom

For 10 years, tea has been growing in the warm balmy climate of the Tregothnan Estate in Cornwall at the extreme south-western tip of Britain. Since 1335, the vast estate has belonged to the Boscawen family and the interest in unusual and exotic plants has been handed down through the generations. Ornamental camellias (*Camellia japonica*) have been grown in the open here for two hundred years and the first experimental seedlings of *Camellia sinensis* were planted at Tregothnan in 1996. Jonathan Jones, Operations Director at Tregothnan, always felt that, although the British climate is generally too harsh for the tea bush, the temperate Cornish air would suit the plants. An old saying states that "Cornwall doesn't have a winter, just a languid spring!" and with temperatures always a little higher than in other parts of Britain, it can

Tregothnan Estate in spring.

feel rather like the higher regions of Darjeeling. In 1999, 8.1 hectares (20 acres) of sheltered valley were cleared and the first seedlings, imported from various tea-growing regions around the world, were planted out and since then a new section of the estate has been cleared and planted to increase the total area to 12.1 hectares (30 acres). Thirty or so different clonal varietals now produce a steady crop through the growing season from March to November and the estate produces both green and black teas and an Earl Grey flavoured with the citrus fruit bergamot which is also grown at Tregothnan. The best of the teas are produced in the late spring. The long-term plan is to develop the business slowly and to maintain a focus on quality and sustainability so that there is a tea estate here in centuries to come. There are also plans to establish an International Tea Centre here, with a tea factory, tea rooms, shops and facilities for conferences, training and exhibitions.

Jonathan Jones, Operations Director at Tregothnan Estate, in the old kitchen garden where the tea now grows.

Tregothnan Classic

Character
This is a mahogany brown, broken orthodox leaf with an attractive scattering of golden tip. The liquor is clear and vibrant copper, the aroma is warm and sweet like molten brown sugar and the taste is robust and invigorating, warming and comforting.

Brewing Tips
Brew 2.5–3g (0.09–0.10oz) in 200ml (7fl oz) of boiling water for 3 minutes.

Tregothnan Classic cup

Tregothnan Classic dry

Leaves withering at Tregothnan prior to rolling.

Tregothnan Classic wet

Tregothnan Afternoon

Character
Oaky brown broken leaf with green and gold tippy flecks yields a deep amber liquor that is similar to a light Darjeeling, and has a soft fruity aroma and taste – perfect afternoon tea to complement traditional tea-time treats.

Brewing Tips
Brew 2.5g (0.09oz) in 200ml (7fl oz) of near boiling water for 2–3 minutes.

Tregothnan Afternoon cup

Tregothnan Afternoon dry

Tregothnan Afternoon wet

Tregothnan Green

Character
A lightly curled blend of China green with Tregothnan leaf gives a liquor that is apricot gold, a sweet floral aroma and a lightly herbal taste with buttery, slightly grassy undertones.

Brewing Tips
Brew 2.5g (0.09oz) in 200ml (7fl oz) water at 85°C (185°F) for 3 minutes.

Tregothnan Green cup

Tregothnan Green dry

Tregothnan Green wet

United States of America

The Americans first tried to grow tea in the nineteenth century on Wadmalaw Island off the coast of South Carolina. After a brief ownership, in 1987 Lipton sold its Charleston Tea Plantation to a private company that produced 'American Classic Tea'. In 2003, the American tea company, Bigelow, purchased the estate and has renamed it Charleston Tea Gardens. Today, visitors can take a trolley ride through 16.2 hectares (40 acres) or so of the plantation to see the bushes growing and then, in the state-of-the-art tea factory, they can watch tea being manufactured from the green leaf stage through to the packaging of the dried black tea. There is also a shop selling the various grades of teas made at different times during the season at the plantation, Bigelow

The mechanical harvester at Charleston Tea Plantation in South Carolina.

Teas, books, tea wares, tea accessories and skin care products (Glycerine Hand Therapy – Body Silk and Hand & Shower Cleansing Gel) whose ingredients include Charleston tea.

In May 2007, planting of tea seedlings also began on 818 hectares (2,021 acres) on the island of Kauai in Hawaii where private housing and tea, cocoa and taro crops have been established side by side. The tea bushes are growing at 130m (425ft) above sea level and will be ready for harvesting in 2009. At full capacity, the total crop is expected to reach approximately 300 tonnes (295 tons). Types of tea to be manufactured here will include speciality green, oolong, white and black and there will be a visitor centre where tourists and local residents will be able to learn more about tea manufacture and shop for the local tea and tea-related items.

Kauai Island in Hawaii where tea was planted for the first time in 2007.

Charleston First Flush

Character
The choppy, quite fibrous leaf brews to give a rich red liquor, which has a sweet biscuity aroma and is sweet and light.

Brewing Tips
Brew 2.5g (0.09oz) in 200ml (7fl oz) of boiling water for 3 minutes.

Charleston First Flush cup

Charleston First Flush dry

Charleston First Flush wet

Vietnam

Tea has been grown in Vietnam for more than 3,000 years, and, as in China, ancient trees that stand several metres high can still be found. The Vietnamese people have a tea-drinking culture that is as colourful and fascinating as that of the Chinese and the serving and sharing of tea is an important part of family, social and business life.

Commercial production started in the 1820s when the French established the first major plantations and in the past few years, the areas under tea have expanded rapidly from 5,400 hectares (13,344 acres) in 1975 to over 80,000 hectares (1,976,800 acres) today. After the disruption of the Vietnam war, foreign investment helped to rehabilitate the plantations and refurbish the factories and output has gone up from 40,000 tonnes (39,368 tons) in 1995 to the current figure of more than 80,000 tonnes (78,737 tons). The major growing regions are in the centre and the north of the country in provinces such as Tuyen Quang, Yen Bai, Phu

Removing the stamens from the lotus flowers for the modern method of flavouring green tea.

Tho, Son La, Ha Giang and Thai Nguyen and the industry is split into a growing number of private companies and joint ventures and a decreasing number of state-owned plantations and factories. Producers have been working steadily to modernize factories and increase capacity in order to meet growing domestic and export demands and Vietnam is today the world's ninth largest tea exporter. The industry plans to triple tea exports by 2010.

The season begins in April each year and the plucked leaf is turned into approximately 80,000 tonnes (78,737 tons) of tea including orthodox and CTC black, steamed and pan-fried greens, flavoured jasmine teas, oolongs and puerhs. The bulk of the green teas are consumed domestically and black varieties are mostly exported. The most special of the Vietnamese teas are the lotus-flavoured teas made traditionally by enclosing small quantities of tea inside the blossoms of lotus flowers overnight so that the tea absorbs the gentle sweet flavour of the flowers' perfume.

Gathering lotus flowers.

Thai Nguyen Green

Character
A traditional green tea from the mountains of Thai Nguyen are made by skilful pan-frying to de-enzyme the leaf, rolling and oven roasting. The resulting slender, elegantly twisted, jade leaf yields a silky, fragrant golden liquor with subtle hints of fennel and toasted wheat with a slightly bitter-sweet aftertaste.

Brewing Tips
Brew 2.5–3g (0.09–0.10oz) in 200ml (7fl oz) water at 75°C (167°F) for 3 minutes. Strain and add more water for a second infusion.

Thai Nguyen cup

Thai Nguyen dry

Thai Nguyen wet

Ancient Lotus

The lotus is a symbol of eternity and good fortune, beauty and purity and the flower has long been used to scent high-grade green tea. Originally created for King Tu Duc during the days of the Nguyen Dynasty, his servants would row across a lake to the place in the water where the lotus grew. They carefully peeled back the fragile petals of the blossoms and placed a small handful of green tea leaves inside. Then they closed the petals tightly around the tea and bound each bloom so that it kept the tea safe and dry overnight while absorbing the flower's scent. The next morning, the servants rowed back out to the lotus, opened the flowers and gathered up the tea ready for the king's breakfast refreshment.

This grade of Lotus tea is perfumed using this traditional method of wrapping small quantities of green tea inside lotus blossoms. The flowers are picked just as they have bloomed, the petals are very carefully peeled back so that a small opening is made through which about 2g (0.07oz) of fresh green tea is placed. The petals are then closed around the tea and bound lightly with threads to hold them in place. The buds are left for 24 hours and then the blossoms are once again opened and the tea extracted. To make 1kg (2.2lb) of tea, 500 lotus flowers are required.

Character
Tightly twisted, wiry, jade green leaves give a pale amber liquor that has a crisp clean flavour and the heady vanilla-sweet perfume of the lotus flower.

Brewing Tips
Brew 2.5–3g (0.09–0.10oz) in 200ml (7fl oz) water at 75–80°C (167–176°F) for 3 minutes. Strain and add more water for two more infusions.

Ancient Lotus cup

Ancient Lotus dry

Ancient Lotus wet

Lotus Blossom

The ancient traditional way of scenting teas inside lotus blossoms is gradually dying out and more modern methods are being used that layer the stamens of the flower heads with the green tea so that the perfume is gradually absorbed.

Character
The neat twists of dark green leaves yield a crystal clear, golden liquor that has a clean, slightly aniseedy flavour and a hint of bitterness in the lingering aftertaste.

Brewing Tips
Brew 2.5–3g (0.09–0.10oz) in 200ml (7fl oz) water at 65–75°C (149–167°F) for 2–3 minutes. Strain and add more water for a further one or two infusions.

Lotus Blossom cup

Lotus Blossom dry

Lotus Blossom wet

Black tea

Vietnamese Marble Mountain

The tea is named after the five mountains to the south of Da Nang. An ancient Vietnamese legend tells how, thousands of years ago, a dragon emerged from the sea and laid an egg on Non Nuoc beach. After 1000 days and nights, the shell began to crack open and a beautiful girl stepped out. Fragments of the shell were transformed into five marble mountains that were named by the king of the Nguyen Dynasty after the five elements.

Character

High grown and full of golden tips, this black Vietnamese tea gives a rich, coppery infusion that has a sweet, slightly spicy aroma and a smooth, sweet, slightly woody, earthy character that is somewhat similar to that of black teas from China.

Brewing Tips

Brew 2.5–3g (0.09–0.10oz) in 200ml (7fl oz) of boiling water for 3–4 minutes.

Vietnamese Marble Mountain cup

Vietnamese Marble Mountain dry

Vietnamese Marble Mountain wet

Other tea-producing countries

Argentina

Argentina has been producing tea since the 1950s, mainly in the Misiones region in the north-east of the country and today exports approximately 50 million kg each year. Because of a shortage of labour, all the harvesting is carried out by large tractor-like machines which trundle between the rows of tea bushes. The teas give a dark liquor that has a plain, somewhat earthy taste and medium body and the majority of exports go to the US for the manufacture of iced tea.

Tea harvesters in Misiones, Argentina.

Australia

First attempts at tea-growing were in the late 1800s but plants were washed away by a cyclone and tidal wave and no further attempts were made to grow tea commercially until 1959. In 1978, a new company, Madura Tea Estates, was established to grow tea in New South Wales. A mixture of both the Assam and Chinese variety of the tea plant is cultivated and the organically grown teas are generally blended with quality organic Ceylons and Assams to create a range of black, green and flavoured teas. The Nerada Tea Company markets tea grown on smallholder farms in the Nerada Valley of northern Queensland. After a major expansion programme into the Cairns Highlands in the 1980s, the company now produces 6 million kg of fresh leaf from 405 hectares (1000 acres) of land and the leaf is processed at the company's factory at Glen Allyn and packed in Brisbane.

Azerbaijan

The total area under tea in the Lankaran–Astara and Zagatala regions of the country has decreased from 13,000 hectares (32,124 acres) in 1999 to approximately 7000 hectares (17,297 acres) today but in 2002, Azerbaijani tea won a gold prize at an international competition held in Madrid. Lankaran region has five tea factories and one packing factory. Domestic consumption is high and most of the tea drunk is imported.

Azores

Although there are no records to prove it, tea is believed to have been introduced to the Azores in 1750. Initial trials for commercial production started in the 1820s when seed from Brazil was planted at Calhetas, Santo Antonio and Calepas. The industry grew very slowly until the 1960s when tea production had risen to 300 tonnes (295 tons) cultivated on 300 hectares (741 acres). In 1984, the government brought in an expert from Mozambique to the island of San Miguel in order to oversee the establishment of new plantations, the introduction of new plants, and new cultivation and manufacturing processes. About 60 factories gradually closed down and today, the industry is very small with only two factories left in operation – Gorreana, founded in 1883, and Porto Formosa which was reopened in 2001. Most of the tea is sold locally to residents and tourists with a small percentage going to the USA, Canada, Germany and Austria. The teas produced include black (a Pekoe, a broken Orange Pekoe, a broken leaf and 'Moinha'), a strong-flavoured tea made from the parts of the leaf that are most fully oxidized) and a steamed green Hyson.

Burundi

Commercial cultivation of tea started in Burundi in the early 1970s. Initially, production increased at a steady pace but, as in other African states, a history of political instability in the past had a negative impact on the industry. Today, tea is the country's second export, accounting for 4–5 per cent of export earnings, production is increasing and efforts are being made to improve quality. Although privatisation has been discussed, the industry is still totally under state control and the Office de Thé du Burundi (OTB) holds the monopoly on manufacture in five factories.

Cameroon

The Germans took the first tea plants to Cameroon in 1914 and planted them at Tole on the fertile slopes of Mount Cameroon. Tole is situated at a height of 600m (2,000ft) above sea level. Conditions here are ideal but recent unrest at the estate means that what were once excellent quality orthodox black teas are now less readily available.

Democratic Republic of Congo

Black tea is produced in the north-eastern highland region, with an annual production of around just 3,000 tonnes (2,953 tons). Although the government has made attempts to increase production, annual output remains low and has in fact dropped since 1978.

Ecuador

Annually, 1,000 tonnes (984 tons)of tea a year are made on the Te Sangay Tea Estate on the 'wrong' side of a 200m- (650ft-) wide river, 915m (3,000ft) up in a stretch of land between the Andes and the Amazon jungle. After manufacture, the tea has to be transported across the river on trolleys that run along a cable to the road, where lorries load it and take it down to the port of Guayaquil.

Ethiopia

Ethiopia is relatively new to tea-growing. First experiments were carried out in the 1930s and since 1978, 2,200 hectares (5,435 acres) have been planted on two state-owned plantations at Wush Wush and Gumero, with further plantings and new factories planned. Until 1989, teas from elsewhere in Africa and China were imported to meet the domestic need but the government established national plantations to help reduce imports. The teas are now beginning to find customers in the European marketplace.

Iran

Since the early 1900s, Iran has been producing tea in the northern provinces of Gilan and Mazandaran. There are 57,000 local households now growing tea and selling their green leaf to 134 processing plants that manufacture black teas. The teas give a reddish, light, smooth liquor.

Italy

For hundreds of years, the Cattolica family of Sant-Andrea di Compito has been growing Camellias and in the 1980s, botanist Guido Cattolica started working with the Lucca (Tuscany) Botanical Garden to produce tea in a new experimental tea garden on the family property. Green teas are produced by the Japanese method of steaming, drying and rolling and Cattolica is now experimenting with oolongs.

Madagascar

The island's clonal teas are grown at a height of 1,675m (5,500ft) on the Sahambavy tea plantation. The manufactured black teas give a bright coloured tea similar to the best East African teas. Production is seasonal, with growth slowing during the dry season of May to September.

Mauritius

Tea was first introduced to the island of Mauritius in the late 1760s by Frenchman Pierre Poivre. Since commercial production started in the 1960s, the Mauritius Tea Factories Company has been established to manage four factories owned by the Tea Development Authority. Economic pressures, high costs and high world tea prices have created problems for the industry. However, cultivation is continuing on small plots of land, leaves are plucked by hand early in the morning and processed by orthodox manufacturing methods. The black teas have a full flavour comparable to English Breakfast type liquors and combine strength with delicacy and an attractive fragrance.

Mozambique

Tea is grown in the agricultural Zambezi region of the country but production has declined over the past 30 years due to political unrest. The strong black teas are generally used in blends for teabags.

Papua New Guinea

Conditions of both climate and soil in Papua New Guinea are ideal for tea and the plant has been grown in the Western Highlands here since the 1800s. The mostly black teas are sold abroad for use in blends.

Russia

Cultivation goes back to 1833 when tea seeds were planted at Nikity Botanical Garden in the Crimea.

After World War II, the industry expanded rapidly. The growing area is in Krasnodar province in the southwest of the country but production is low and quality poor.

South Africa

The first tea plants, brought from Kew Gardens in London, were planted in 1850 in Durban Botanical Gardens, Natal. Commercial cultivation started in 1877 using seeds from Assam and estates were then planted out in Kwa-Zulu-Natal (1959), in the Drakensberg Mountains in Eastern Transvaal, in other parts of Natal, in Transkei (1960s), in the Levubu area, in Venda and in central Zululand near Ntingwe (from 1973). However, the high costs of labour in recent times has led to the closure of all but the Kwa-Zulu-Natal plantations. Leaf is harvested during the short rainy season from November to March and most is processed into black tea by a modified CTC method. South Africa is also now famous for the production of Rooibos (also known as Rositea or Red Tea), which is processed from the leaf of *Aspalathus linearis*, not from *Camellia sinensis*.

Tanzania

German settlers were the first to grow tea at Amari and Rungwa in the early 1900s. Commercial production started in 1926 and the industry expanded steadily in the Southern Highlands and the Usambaras. The industry operates on two levels – private estates that grow and manufacture their own tea and smallholder farmers who sell their leaf to state-owned factories run by the Tanzania Tea Authority. Production varies from year to year depending on labour shortages, transportation problems, weather patterns, etc, and quality varies according to altitude and plucking standards. The black teas produced are all good-quality CTC and fetch average prices on world markets.

Tibet

Tibet has grown tea since the days of China's Tang Dynasty (AD 618–906) and today the All-The-Tea Company produces organic green tea at the Yigong Tea Plantation in Linzhi Prefecture. The plantation lies at an altitude of 3,650m (11,975ft) amongst high mountain peaks where the cool misty conditions are excellent for the tea bushes. Because of the high elevation, the tea is only harvested during one season each year.

Turkey

Since 1938, Turkey has been growing tea in the Rize district close to the Black Sea. The 60,000 farming families and local factories produce medium-grade tea that gives a dark liquor and a gentle, almost sweet flavour. Turkish tea is mostly consumed domestically.

Uganda

Tea was introduced into the Botanic Gardens at Entebbe, Uganda, in 1909 but there was no commercial cultivation until the late 1920s when

Brooke Bond began extensive planting. From the mid–1950s there was rapid expansion and by the early 1970s tea had become the country's most important export. Political instability in the 1970s and '80s brought a major decline but since 1989 a major rehabilitation of the plantations and factories has brought increased output. Ugandan teas are all black and most are exported for use in teabag blends.

Zimbabwe

Tea cultivation started here in the 1960s and there are now two main tea-growing areas – in Chipinge and Honde Valley in the south-east of the country. Rainfall is low, at only about 66cm (26in) a year, whereas 127cm (50in) is required. An efficient irrigation system is essential and the cold winter season means that the bush only grows from spring through to autumn. All the tea produced is black and is mostly exported for blending. Tea quality has gradually been diminishing over the past few years due to the country's unstable financial and political situation under President Mugabe.

Tea plantation in Zimbabwe.

Tea-drinking around the world

The Chinese drink green tea as their national everyday beverage, just as they did centuries ago, and offer a bowlful to all guests upon arrival in the home. In some houses, the traditional 'gongfu' ceremony is performed using a set of delicate tea bowls, straight-sided smelling cups, a small earthenware teapot and the traditional method of making several infusions from the same measure of leaves, each with its own individual aroma and flavour. The same carefully choreographed preparation and serving of tea is also part of life in Chinese retail stores and tea rooms and groups of customers sometimes sit for an hour or more trying different teas brewed carefully by the shop owner before deciding which to buy. Chinese social life still centres around the tea house, where people of all types and ages mingle, drink tea, and catch up with the latest gossip. The different teas are brewed in glasses, guywans or teapots, with additional water often poured onto the same leaves to give several infusions. While groups of friends chat, watch a performance of Beijing Opera, a group of acrobats or musicians, a waiter moves around the room, dispensing more water from a kettle with a long spout.

In Korea, the brewing and serving of tea has close connections with Buddhist monasteries and each element of the ceremony has a spiritual significance and purpose. The ritual prepares and encourages those taking part to enter the quiet

Learning to perform the tea ceremony in Korea.

ceremony with their senses and spirit open to an enjoyment of all the details of each action and an appreciation of the connections between the physical objects – the water, the fire, the teapot and bowls – and his or her place in the world and relationship with other people and the wider universe. The tea master prepares the tea in a small pot and serves it in tiny bowls to the guests who bow to each other before admiring the visual beauty of the liquor, enjoying the aroma and savouring the tea's flavour. Several infusions are made from one measure of leaf and when all the tea has been drunk, the guests again bow to each other and to their host and take their leave.

In China, tea is often drunk from guywans, as in this tea house.

In Mongolia, 'brick' tea (see page 49) is crushed and brewed with water and yak buttermilk, the liquor is then strained and mixed with milk, salt, butter and roasted grain. In Tibet, brick tea is crushed and soaked in water overnight and the infusion is then churned with salt, goat's milk and yak butter to produce a thick buttery drink. Sometimes a handful or two of grain is added to make a nourishing, soup-like food known as 'tsampa'. Both Mongolian and Tibetan tea are drunk from a bowl rather than a cup.

The Russians have always traditionally brewed their tea with a samovar – an urn that developed from the Mongolian cooking stove and that consists of a pot set on top of a tall chimney sitting over a fire (as in Japan and Europe, the local tea-drinkers adapted the method of brewing that they learnt from the Chinese to suit their own cooking methods and equipment). A little pot of black tea is brewed very strong and then placed, to keep warm, on the top of the samovar. When tea is served, a cup is half filled with the strong tea, watered down with hot water drawn from the tap in the side of the samovar, and drunk with sugar or jam.

In Turkey, a strong black brew is prepared and strained into tulip-shaped glasses and served with little sweetmeats. In the eastern part of the country, a cube of sugar is placed under the tongue before the tea is sipped from the glass. Some Turks drink so much tea that they carry a 'semover', like a Russian samovar, in the back of their car so as to always be able to boil water for tea. In domestic

Tea Salon Bara-no-ki (Japanese for Rose Tea), an English-style tea room in Tokyo.

life, tea has great importance; mothers always ensure their daughters know how to brew tea correctly.

In Iran and Afghanistan, tea is the national beverage. Both green and black are used – green as a refreshing thirst quencher and black as a warming, comforting brew, and both types are taken with sugar. At home and in the popular tea houses, drinkers sit cross-legged on floormats and sip their tea from glasses or elegant porcelain bowls.

Moroccans have also drunk tea for centuries, having learnt the custom from early Arab traders, and consider it an important part of any social or business occasion. At a Moroccan tea-drinking ceremony incense is lit, and all those taking part wash their hands in orange blossom water and watch while the host prepares the tea. Green tea, fresh mint and sugar are measured into a tall silver pot and hot water is then poured in. Little glasses are set ready on a tray and when the tea has brewed, the golden liquor is poured from a height so that it froths into the glasses and settles with a layer of tiny bubbles on the surface. Accompanying nibbles include dried apricots, figs and nuts.

In Egypt, the Bedouin version of the drink is made by boiling tea leaves and sweetening the infusion with plenty of sugar. Tea is also flavoured with dried mint leaves and served with sugar in glasses.

In Japan, the traditional Green Tea Ceremony (see pages 10 and 86) is still an important social ritual and the ability to perform it is considered an essential skill for well-educated young ladies. Although the most popular tea is still green, many Japanese today also enjoy black tea drunk in the British way with milk. Since the 1980s, many British-style tea rooms have opened in which traditional afternoon tea is served with sandwiches, scones and clotted cream, and little cakes and pastries. In some metropolitan areas, there are also some very stylish green tea 'cafes' that serve unusual flavoured and blended green teas.

In India, black tea is drunk with milk and sugar. Young boys ('chai wallahs') brew tea on street corners using kettles and brass pots and mix it with buffalo milk and sugar. They sell it to passers-by who drink it from little earthenware cups that are thrown away after use. Spiced tea, known as 'chai' or 'marsala chai' and made with pepper, cinnamon, cardamom, cloves and sugar, is also very popular. 'Afternoon tea', with savoury and sweet snacks, is served in the tea rooms of India's smart hotels throughout the afternoon.

In Sri Lanka, lunchtime tea with 'hoppers' is a traditional institution.

Street sellers of tea in India.

Hoppers are a type of pancake made with rice flour, coconut milk, sugar, salt and yeast and cooked in a special pan to give a bowl shape. They are served with a variety of curries and spicy sauces. In hotels, as in India, 'afternoon tea' is offered throughout the afternoon.

In Malaysia, tea is brewed very strong and then mixed with thick condensed milk and plenty of sugar. Sometimes the tea and condensed milk are mixed together and then poured several times between two jugs so that the liquid becomes deliciously frothy. The Malaysians also like iced tea, made by pouring strong hot tea and condensed milk over crushed ice.

In the UK, black tea is still the preferred brew for most people but consumption of green and flavoured teas is on the increase. Many people start the day with a cup of tea in bed,

Afternoon tea at the Hyatt Regency Churchill, London.

more tea at breakfast and lunch and, increasingly, tea after the main meal in the evening. Afternoon tea at 4pm or 5pm is still a very important institution, with many families serving it at home at the weekend, and all the major hotels around the country offering pots of tea served with neat little sandwiches, scones with jam and cream and a selection of elegant pastries and cakes.

United Kingdom

Amber McCarroll
email: ambermccaroll@hotmail.com
Tasseologist and writer

Betty's Cafe Tea Rooms
1 Parliament Street
Harrogate
North Yorkshire HG1 2QU
Tel: (00 44) (0) 1423 502746
*Traditional tea rooms and tea retailers
with branches across Yorkshire*

Infuse Tea Ltd
19 Roxeth Hill, Harrow-on-the-Hill
Middlesex HA2 0JY
Tel: (00 44) (0) 20 8426 8064/5
Email: asteward@infuse-tea.co.uk
Tea classes for Japanese people in London

Ismail Coffee & Tea
95-97 Mount Pleasant Road
Tunbridge Wells, Kent
TN1 1QG
raschid@ismail.co.uk
www.ismail.co.uk
Tea retail store and tea room

Jane Pettigrew
www.janepettigrew.com
jane.pettigrew@btinternet.com
*Writer, lecturer, trainer, tea masterclasses,
consultant*

Jing Tea Ltd
14 Helix Gardens
London, SW2 2JP
Tel: 020 7183 2113
Contact Ed Eisler or Freddie Bourne
info@jingtea.com
www.jingtea.com
*Wholesale and online store specializing in
Chinese and other teas and tea accessories*

Northern Tea Merchants
Crown House
193 Chatsworth Road
Chesterfield, Derbyshire
S40 2BA
james@northern-tea.com;
rbr75@dial.pipex.com
Tel: (00 44) (0)1246 232600
www.northern-tea.com
*Retail shop, tearoom and online store
selling a wide variety of world teas and
tea accessories*

Nothing But Tea
1 Grisedale Cort
Kempston
Bedford, MK42 7EE
Tel: (00 44) (0) 1234 852121
Fax: (00 44) (0) 1234 853232
Email: info@nbtea.co.uk
www.nbtea.co.uk
*Wholesale and online suppliers of tea and
tea accessories*

Postcard Teas
9 Dering Street, London, W1S 1AG
Tel: 020 7629 3654
info@postcardteas.com
www.postcardteas.com
*Tasting room and retail shop selling teas
from India, Sri Lanka, Taiwan, Korea,
Japan and China*

Teacraft
1 Grisedale Cort, Kempston,
Bedford, MK42 7EE
Tel: (00 44) (0) 1234 852121
Fax: (00 44) (0) 1234 853232
www.teacraft.com
*Consultants and technical advisers to the
world tea industry*

Tregothnan Tea Estate
Tregothnan Estate Office, Truro,
Cornwall, TR2 4AN
Tel: (00 44) (0) 1872 520000
Fax: (00 44) (0) 1872 520583
info@tregothnan.com
www.tregothnan.com
*First British tea plantation;
manufacturers of green and black teas*

The UK Tea Council
9 The Courtyard
Gowan Avenue, London SW6 6RH
Tel: (0044) (0)20 7371 7787
email: tea@teacouncil.co.uk
www.teacouncil.co.uk
*Independent body representing major tea-
producing countries and UK packers;
dedicated to promoting tea*

United States

Elmwood Inn Fine Teas/Benjamin
Press
PO Box 100
Perryville
KY 40468
USA
www.elmwoodinn.com
*Tea retailers and trainers, publishers and
book distributors*

Harney & Sons Fine Teas
PO Box 665
Salisbury, CT 06068
(001) 888–427–6398
www.harney.com
*Retailers and wholesalers of teas from
around the world; tea-related gifts and
books*

Peet's Coffee & Tea
PO Box 12509
Berkeley, CA 94712–3509
(001) 800–999–2132
www.peets.com
*Tea retailers with locations throughout
North America*

Simpson & Vail, Inc
PO Box 765
3 Quarry Rd, Brookfield, CT 06804
(001) 203–775–0240
www.svtea.com
*Tea wholesalers and retailers offering a wide
range of teas, tea-related gifts, books, linens*

The Tao of Tea
3430 S.E. Belmont Street
Portland, Oregon 97214
Tel: (001) 503–736–0198
Fax: (001) 503–736–9232
Email: info@taooftea.com
www.taooftea.com
*Specialists in teas from China, Taiwan,
Vietnam, puerhs, flower-flavoured teas,
accessories*

The Tea House
541 Fessler Avenue
Naperville, IL 60565
(001) 630–961–0877
ddrteaman@aol.com
www.theteahouse.com
*Importers, blenders and retailers of the
world's finest teas and accessories;
specialists in Chinese and Taiwanese teas;*

*organiser of tea tours to different tea
regions of the world*

Tea Source
752 Cleveland Ave. So.
St Paul, MN 55116
(001) 651–690–9822
www.teasource.com
Tea retail counters and tea bars

Teavana
(001) 404–995–8203
www.teavana.com
*Tea bars and retail counters in locations
throughout North America*

Todd and Holland
7311 West Madison Street
Forest Park, IL 60130
(001) 800–747–8327
www.todd-holland.com
Tea retailer

Upton Tea Imports
34-A Hayden
Rowe Street
Hopkinton, MA 01748
(001) 508–435–9922
www.uptontea.com
Tea importers and retailers

Rest of the World

Babingtons
Piazza de Spagna 23
Rome 00187
Italy
Tel: (00 39) 6 67 866 027
*English-style tea room and tea retailer in
the centre of Rome*

Hand Made Tea Makers'
Association of Georgia – Geo Tea Ltd
41 Bakchtrioni str.
Tbilisi 0194
Republic of Georgia
Tel: +995 99 56 31 64
Fax: +995 33 17 66 41
Email: tmikadze@yahoo.com
*Hand- and machine-made teas produced
by local families*

Marco Polo Products Pte Ltd
79 Chitrakoot Building
230-AAJC Bose Road
Calcutta 700 020
Tel: (00 91) 33 2247 1036
Fax: (00 91) 33 2247 7508
email: goomtee@darjeelingteas.com
*Tea planters and wholesalers – owners of
Goomtee and Jungpana estates in
Darjeeling*

Mariage Frères
13 rue des Grands-Augustins
Paris 75006
France
Tel: (00 33) 1 40 51 82 50
*Tea rooms and tea retail counters in three
locations in Paris*

Mount Everest Tea Company GmbH
(Tea and accessories)
Daimlerstrasse 13
Elmshorn
D 25337
Germany
Contact: Christian Draak
C.Draak@mount-everest-tea.de
www.mount-everest-tea.de
Tea and tea accessory wholesaler

Wijs & Zonen
Warmoesstraat 102
1012 JJ Amsterdam
The Netherlands
Tel: (00 31) 20 624 0436
Fax: (00 31) 20 625 6648
email: info@wijs-zonen.nl
Speciality tea merchants

Inproc
Denneweg 126
2514 CL Den Haag
The Netherlands
Tel: (00 31) 70 346 1541
email: inproc@koffietuin.nl
Speciality tea merchants

Fa.wed.A.Garsen – de Pelikaan
Pelikaanstraat 9
7201 DR Zutphen
The Netherlands
Tel: (00 31) 575 512 024
Fax: (00 31) 575 541 750
email: pelikaan-
wed.a.garsen@planet.nl

Simon Lévelt Koffiebranderij en
Theehandel
A. Hofmanweg 3
2031 BH Haarlem
Tel: (00 31) 235 122 522

Fax: (00 31) 235 122 505
www.simonlevelt.com
*28 speciality shops covering most major
Dutch towns*

Cameron Highlands Resort
Malaysia
www.cameronhighlandsresort.com
*Hotel and spa in Malaysia's tea-
producing region of the Cameron
Highlands*

Sri Lanka
Tea-related holiday resorts
Tea Trails
www.teatrails.com
*Four planters bungalows surrounded by
high-altitude tea plantations, refurbished
as luxury holiday homes*

The Tea Factory, Kandapola, Nuwara
Eliya
www.aitkenspencehotels.lk/teafactory
/home.shtml
*What was once a tea processing factory is
now a hotel set at an altitude of 2,073m
(6,800 ft) in the highest tea-growing
region of the island*

Thailand
Thai Tea Suwirun
info@thaiteasuwirun.com
Tea company and online sales

Index

Page numbers in **bold** indicate main entries in the Directory section. Page numbers in *italic* indicate an illustration.